INSTRUCTOR'S MANUAL

to accompany

Reading Across the Disciplines
College Reading and Beyond

Third Edition

Prepared By
Mary Dubbé
And
Susan Pongratz
Thomas Nelson Community College

New York Boston San Francisco
London Toronto Sydney Tokyo Singapore Madrid
Mexico City Munich Paris Cape Town Hong Kong Montreal

Instructor's Manual to accompany McWhorter, *Reading Across the Disciplines: College Reading and Beyond,* third edition.

ISBN: 0-321-44581-3

2 3 4 5 6 7 8 9 10–OPM–09 08 07

Table of Contents

Part I: Handbook

Part II: Readings in Academic Disciplines

Part III: Textbook Chapter Readings

Part IV: Useful Teaching Materials

Part V: Answer Keys

Part VI: Appendix   301

GUIDE FOR INSTRUCTORS

Introduction

"Plato believed that all learning is remembering what we have forgotten."
Madeleine L'Engle

The students in your developmental English class are the people who run the world. They are bank tellers and office managers. They make phone calls for telemarketers and serve fast food. They wait tables and style hair. They fix cars, work retail, and guard lives in swimming pools. Students are in your class for a myriad of reasons. Some want to learn strategies to become the competition; some are there because they need 12 hours to stay on their parents' insurance policy. Others may be ESL students and want to improve their English, and some want to become better parents and proactive citizens. Many hope to learn the skills to get a better job. Also, the students in your developmental English class learn in many ways. They use visual, auditory, kinesthetic, or a combination of learning styles. Some are afraid. And they are in your class despite those fears. They have great courage.

This text was written in response to the need for developing reading as an essential skill needed for success in college courses, and providing sufficient opportunity for practice and application. Its unique features are described in the following sections.

Emphasis on Reading in the Disciplines

Reading is an integration of learned behaviors, skills, attitudes, and personal resources that results in the understanding, interpretation, and evaluation of printed materials, as well as the application of its content. As such, it is a complex task influenced simultaneously by numerous factors. By the time they enter college, most students have acquired a foundation of reading skills; they have acquired basic word-recognition skills, phonetic and structural analysis skills, and a functioning level of comprehension skills that allow them to understand and recall textual material. However, most college students have not developed the spectrum of skills and abilities that is needed to handle the level of sophisticated reading characteristic of college textbooks. They read relatively slowly and have difficulty comprehending and recalling difficult material. They frequently lose concentration and have to reread. Most students have one general approach to reading and lack strategies to apply to the various college disciplines. The emphasis throughout this text, then, is the development of reading skills necessary for success in content-area courses.

Emphasis on Academic Reading

The text focuses on the reading skills students need to handle their academic coursework. General reading skills, such as literal comprehension, vocabulary development, and critical reading skills, are taught in handbook format through brief skills instruction. Exercises follow using sample textbook paragraphs or articles of longer length.

Chapter 10 introduces the need to adjust reading and thinking skills needed for success in the various academic disciplines.

Part Two contains three reading selections from 12 different academic disciplines (including the hard sciences and more contemporary concerns of public life), three selections based on the world of work, and two complete textbook chapters for students to practice the application of the skills they have learned. Students are also given tips and strategies for successful reading in each of the disciplines. These skills are then reinforced through extensive practice structured around the readings. Finally, two complete textbook chapters (one from a psychology text and one from a biology text) are provided to enable students to practice skills on longer pieces of writing.

Reading as Thinking

Metacognitive Strategies

Metacognition, a learner's awareness of his or her own cognitive processes, is a current topic of interest in verbal learning and reading comprehension research. There is strong evidence that mature and proficient readers exert a great deal of cognitive control over their own reading and learning processes by analyzing tasks, selecting appropriate learning strategies, and monitoring their effectiveness. Less proficient students tend to make fewer decisions about the task and have little awareness of their reading processes and outcomes. Throughout this text students are encouraged to develop metacognitive strategies, focusing on task analysis, selecting appropriate strategies, and evaluation.

Thought Patterns/Organizational Structure

Research has established that awareness of organizational patterns and textual structure facilitates comprehension and recall. This text describes in detail six organizational patterns (Chapter 4) that appear frequently in textbook writing and four additional patterns that are useful in academic writing. These patterns, presented as organizing schema, are used to provide meaning and structure to text and class assignments. Part Two provides selections from various academic disciplines offering extensive practice in analyzing these patterns.

Writing as Learning

A recent focus within many academic disciplines is the use of writing as a learning and discovery process. While students accept writing as a vehicle of communication, few are proficient in its use as a means of organizing thought, focusing ideas, recognizing relations, or generating new ideas. Chapter 7 examines writing as a learning process and presents numerous writing-to-learn strategies, including annotating, outlining, paraphrasing, mapping, and summarizing.

Research evidence has established that awareness of text structure facilitates comprehension and recall. Several chapters in the text focus on structure.

Chapter 3 is concerned with paragraph structure. Chapter 4 discusses six common thought patterns: definition, classification, order or sequence, cause-and-effect, and comparison-and-contrast. Part Two of the text emphasizes the structure and organization of textbooks in twelve disciplines and in the workplace.

Integration of Reading And Writing

Since reading and writing are complementary psycholinguistic processes, an effort has been made throughout the text to emphasize this relationship and to provide practice in both. Students are often called on to respond to exercises by writing sentences or brief paragraphs. In addition, each of the reading selections in Part Two provides open-ended literal and critical-reading questions that require written responses. Discussion questions are provided for all reading selections. These may be used as writing assignments or as collaborative learning exercises.

Active Learning

Many university classrooms seem to have forgotten that learning is naturally an active process. Active learning involves putting students in situations which compel them to read, speak, listen, think deeply, and write. Active learning puts the responsibility of organizing what is to be learned in the hands of the learners themselves, and ideally lends itself to a more diverse range of learning. Chapter 7 focuses on methods to enable students to become active readers and learners. Students then have a wealth of opportunity to practice these skills in the selected readings from the various disciplines in Part Two of the text. In addition each of the selections requires the students to select a learning strategy appropriate for the discipline and the reading.

Visual and Electronic Literacy

One measure of success for today's college students is their ability to effectively use the vast resources available on the Internet. Chapter 9, "Reading and Evaluating Electronic Sources," guides students in understanding how electronic text is different from print text and how to use Web sites to gather information. In addition students are taught how to evaluate the purpose, content, accuracy, and structure of the Web site. Every reading selection in Part Two also includes additional Web sites for students to explore that relate to each reading. Although every effort has been made to ensure that current, accurate, appropriate sites have been listed, please remember to check them first before offering them to students as Follow-Up work. (As an instructor, you may want to check out the following: www.turnitin.com, which is a site to apprise you of plagiarism, and www.pinkmonkey.com, which offers "on-line Cliff Notes" for student use.

Balance Between Rate and Comprehension

Many basic reading texts emphasize the development of literal comprehension skills; others, commonly known as speed reading texts, emphasize rate increase. This text, unlike the others, treats rate and comprehension as interactive variables in the effort to produce efficient and flexible readers. Reading rate is approached as a variable that, along with others, must be controlled or manipulated according to the academic discipline and nature of the text in order to produce the desired result. Many students feel that a low reading rate is at the core of their reading problem, and that if only they could learn to read faster, their problems would be solved. Actually, low reading rate is more often a symptom than a problem in itself.

In explaining the balance between rate and comprehension to students, it is useful to present rate and comprehension as tradeoffs, much like price and quality in the purchase of consumer goods. Many slow readers do not realize that reading at a low rate often indicates comprehension difficulty; that they read slowly because of this. One effective way to explain this relationship is to use the analogy of a fever. A fever ordinarily suggests that something else is wrong in the body, an infection or body malfunction. The fever is a symptom of a problem, but it is not the cause. Similarly, a low reading rate often suggests that the reader is experiencing some other reading difficulty. With college readers, the problem is most often literal comprehension skills. However, for a student functioning at eight-grade level or below, for example, the problem may be traced to lack of word recognition, phonetic analysis, or word-meaning acquisition skills. While discipline-related vocabulary is stressed throughout the text, no attempt is made in this text to include instructional units on word recognition, phonics, or core vocabulary development because a student who lacks these basic skills is not ready to handle other skills developed throughout this text.

Vocabulary Development

A basic knowledge of word meanings is at the root of understanding academic writing. Unless a student has a working knowledge and control of a vocabulary, he or she will not be able to comprehend the sophisticated level of writing that is typical of the academic disciplines. Comprehension diminishes as confusion over word meanings arises; rate fluctuates as the reader encounters unknown words.

Because of its importance in the overall development of mature reading behaviors, vocabulary is discussed early in the text. Chapter 2 employs a practical approach to vocabulary development (understanding context clues and analyzing word structure clues) because few students have the time or desire to undertake an extensive program of word study. Practical methods for strengthening word power are presented and easily developed skills are suggested.

Each reading selection also includes a vocabulary exercise, thereby maintaining an emphasis on vocabulary throughout the text as well as helping students to become familiar with the vocabulary associated with the various academic disciplines. Each vocabulary exercise emphasizes the use of context clues and word parts to obtain meaning.

Critical Reading Skills

The abilities to interpret, evaluate, and apply what one reads to real-life situations are essential for an active, mature reader. A vital aspect in the development of a successful college reader, then, is acquisition of critical reading skills. Too often students and content-area instructors alike assume that literal comprehension and recall (the careful, complete understanding of actual content) are all that are needed. Both often fail to recognize the need to interpret, assess, evaluate, and criticize written materials. Chapter 6 of the text is devoted to developing several essential critical reading skills, including distinguishing fact from opinion, identifying purpose, distinguishing tone, detecting bias, and using figurative language. Each of the reading selections in Part Two includes a section based on thinking critically.

Interchangeable Instructional Units

Many instructors have developed preferred instructional sequences that are particularly effective for the type of course they teach and well suited to the needs of their students. Because of this preference, the chapters of this book are interchangeable rather than sequentially dependent. Instructors, then, are not limited to teaching the skills in the order in which they are presented.

Reading Selections

Thirty-nine reading selections and two complete textbook chapters follow the handbook of skills in Part Two. These selections can be used in a variety of ways.

1. Because the selections vary widely in content, organization, and style, an instructor may choose the selection that is more appropriate to the interest level, reading level, major fields of study, age, or cultural diversity of the class.

2. Recognizing that student motivation is crucial to learning, an instructor may allow students to choose which selection they will read in each chapter.

3. One selection may serve as a class exercise during which the instructor discusses technique and monitors and evaluates the students. The second and third may be completed by each student independently as a reinforcement or Follow-Up exercise.

4. If only one selection is used to complete in-chapter assignments, the second and third can be used in several ways. First, an instructor may return to unused selections at a later time for additional skill practice or reinforcement. Second, unused selections may be assigned to advanced students who seem eager for skill applications. Finally, unused readings maybe individually assigned to students who exhibit a specific skill deficiency and who would benefit from additional guided practice.

In essence, the choice of three selections provides the instructor and the student with flexibility and alternatives.

1. *Multiple-Choice Format*

Multiple-choice questions follow each reading selection in Part Two. Understanding the thesis and main ideas (A) and identifying details (B) cover both literal and interpretive comprehension skills. Sections (C) and (D) measure ability to analyze the pattern of organization used in the reading and the ability to organize ideas. Sections (E) and (F) provide practice in determining inferred meanings and thinking critically. Section (G) provides practice in using context clues and word parts to determine word meaning. Because the multiple-choice questions are structured systematically throughout the text, they permit the student and the instructor to evaluate error patterns and to determine areas of strength and weakness.

2. *Open-Ended Format*

Open-ended questions follow the multiple-choice questions that provide practice in selecting a learning/study strategy, exploring ideas through discussion and writing, and exploring related sites on the Web (Sections H, I, and J). These questions are intended to provide an opportunity for the integration of reading and writing skills, provoke and stimulate thought, and encourage discussion and/or collaborative learning.

Practice Exercises

Many students need help in applying and transferring skills. Often the mere presentation of a technique is not sufficient. Students require a number of situations with which they can experiment, practice, and apply skills that have been presented. To help meet this need, two types of practice exercises are included in the text:

1. in-chapter exercises on each reading skill presented in Part One
2. integrated exercises based on reading selections from academic disciplines in Part Two

The in-chapter exercises are constructed to provide immediate practice and allow the student to measure a skill as it is being taught. They also give the student immediate feedback on the various techniques and skills. The exercises based on the reading selections encourage students to integrate all the skills taught in the handbook. In these exercises, students are given the opportunity to apply techniques to materials specifically chosen for the academic disciplines. In addition, exercises based on two complete textbook chapters are offered to give students practice with longer selections more typical of their content- area courses.

General Suggestions for Teaching the Course

Structuring the Course

Classroom Arrangement

A comfortable, nonthreatening classroom environment is most suitable for instruction. The arrangement, however, should have enough structure to encourage students to approach the class seriously and attentively. It is useful to arrange the seating so that the instructor can readily observe each student as he or she reads.

Class Scheduling

Because regular practice, frequent repetition, and reinforcement of skills are needed, frequent class meetings are necessary. At least two class sessions per week are needed; three or four sessions per week are desirable.

Student Conferences

At the beginning of the semester, scheduling individual conferences is an effective way to become acquainted with each student and his or her individual needs. During the conference, you can make sure that the course is appropriate for the student and begin to identify the student's individual strengths and weaknesses. The conference also offers a good opportunity to review the results of any reading or achievement tests that may have been used in placing the student in or recommending him or her for the course.

Students respond extremely favorably to the opportunity to meet with the instructor individually. Students with reading problems are eager to discuss their problem with someone, and students who want to further develop their reading skills welcome the occasion to discuss their particular profile of skills.

Many instructors use the initial conference to get a verbal commitment from the student, i.e., an acknowledgment that he or she is interested in the course and plans to approach it seriously. A student who is committed to the course feels obligated to attend, participate in class, and apply the skills learned to other courses.

Periodic progress-check conferences are useful throughout the semester to help motivate the student, provide feedback on his or her progress, check whether he or she is applying the skills taught to other materials, and encourage him or her to do so.

An end-of-the course evaluation conference can be scheduled to review the student's work, discuss any end-of-semester test results, and suggest areas for further study.

Attendance Policy

Regular class attendance should be emphasized. If college policy permits, an attendance requirement or maximum number of allowable absences should be established at the beginning of the course. Students can seldom develop the skills presented and discussed in class on their own. Also, many students need the direction and structure that an attendance policy provides. While discussing your attendance policy with the students, you might suggest that if they could learn the skills necessary for rigorous academic courses on their own, they would have done so already and would not need to attend class.

If college policy does not allow you to establish an attendance policy, an alternative is to structure the grading system so that regular class attendance is necessary to complete in class assignments or take weekly quizzes or mastery tests.

Credit/Noncredit

Always an important issue in regard to any type of reading-study course is the awarding of degree credit for course completion. Although many colleges grant credit for such a course, some do not; several others award credit but do not accept it toward the fulfilling of degree requirements.

When a particular institution does not give degree credit for the course, the reason usually given is that remedial work does not deserve college credit. Students, of course, argue vehemently that they do as much work and learn as much in a reading-study course as in other courses they take. Often, the issue of credit can influence student motivation and performance. If your institution will not award credit, a strategy to change this policy is to offer the course as noncredit at first. Then, as the course is taught, document new skills learning that occurs and show that students are learning techniques that they were never taught previously. Also, retain records of the number of hours of student work required and the assignments given. These materials will be useful if the department decides at some point to submit the course for credit.

Grading Policy

A grading system is difficult to establish for a reading-study course. As for any other college course, there are advantages and disadvantages to most grading systems. A number of options, and their pros and cons, are summarized below.

1. **Traditional quizzes and exams**. There are true/false quizzes and multiple-choice tests already prepared in the test manual for each of the ten chapters in the handbook. These provide an objective evaluation of the student's progress, and they measure the student's ability to recall facts, principles, and techniques taught. They can be used in any of the following ways:

- An unannounced quiz at the beginning of class. (These points could be added as bonus points to chapter tests as a way to reward students for being prepared. See "To the Instructor," p. 5, *Test Bank.*)

- A pre-test to determine students' prior knowledge. (This will give students an opportunity to see the relevancy of the material and an opportunity for the instructor to determine how much background and preparation are needed.)

- A post-test to measure the students' knowledge of the skills introduced. (Both students and instructor can then assess if further work needs to be done. This is an opportunity to individualize the course for each student.)

2. **Skill application quizzes and exams.** These tests are constructed to measure how effectively a student can perform a skill as it is applied to the actual setting of an academic course. Testing that approximates practical-use situations gives the students real practice in demonstrating that he or she has learned the skills and techniques, thus making the course much more relevant. Each of the ten chapters in Part One contains two skill-based mastery tests using actual college-text excerpts. Three discipline-based tests have been composed for each of the academic disciplines featured in Part Two of the text as well as for the complete psychology and history chapters. Finally, to provide more opportunities for skills-application practice, two additional disciplinary tests have been composed for each discipline using more excepts from college textbooks. Students have many opportunities to learn the skills needed to be successful in their academic courses.

These tests can be used in any of the following ways:

- An unannounced quiz at the beginning of class to reward students for being prepared. (See "To the Instructor," p. 5, *Test Bank.*)

- A post-test to measure the students' knowledge of discipline-specific skills, ability to apply them, and comprehension of college-level text. (Instructors can assess how well the students are able to apply the reading skills learned in the chapter to college-level reading. Both students and instructor can then assess if further work needs to be done. This is an excellent opportunity to individualize the course for each student by recommending supplemental work. See last section of test manual, "Disciplinary Skill-Based Mastery Tests.")

- A group project to encourage collaboration.

3. **The contract system.** A contract system is frequently used in skill courses in which the amount of application and practice is crucial to learning. Contracts can be established with a class as a whole or with students individually. A class contract details the amount of work and the assignments a student must complete

in order to earn a grade of A, B, or C. An individual student contract that focuses on areas in which the student needs further work and additional practice can be written. A student who has difficulty identifying main ideas, for instance, will also have difficulty outlining, mapping, and summarizing. A contract could be devised in which the student completes additional practice in identifying main ideas and further work in outlining, mapping, and summarizing. The individual student contract is particularly workable with the variety of selections offered in this text.

Student Records

Many instructors find it useful to keep a file folder for each student in which is kept all the student's work: assignments, tests, and grading contracts, as well as any additional handouts or worksheets distributed in class. The folders should be brought to each class session and distributed at the beginning of class. Instructors who use this system find that it is convenient to have all materials readily available to be used for reference, Follow-Up, or examples. If the organization of course materials is left completely to the students, instructors find that many of them come to class without the materials which the instructor wishes to use.

Bringing Textbook to Class

At the beginning of the semester, you will avoid much frustration if you insist that each student always bring the textbook to class.

Organizing the Course Content

The text is structured into self-contained sections, or parts, to permit flexibility in organizing course content. Depending on the type of student, the priority which individual instructors place on particular skills, and the time during the semester that the course is offered, may instructors have strong preferences about what skills should be taught first and how skills should be sequenced. Instructors are encouraged to use the text as best suits their individual needs.

Specific suggestions for organizing and structuring course content are offered below.

Skill Orientation

It is important to establish the course as skill-oriented and to emphasize that performance, not acquisition of knowledge, is the criterion of success. The overall goal of the course is to enable the students to apply the skills successfully to their academic courses.

Tightly Structuring the Course

Many students enrolled in a reading course require organization and structure in order to feel comfortable. They are often confused by a loosely structured or flexible course organization in which course objectives are unclear. The following suggestions may be useful in helping students understand the organization and structure of the course:

1. **Distribute a syllabus listing the agenda**. Before classes begin, instructors usually plan out what they will teach each week throughout the semester. Students respond well if the instructor shares the semester's plan with them. They like to know what to expect and what the course will include. A syllabus, listing the skill(s) to be covered each week, with corresponding dates, can easily be prepared from your own plans. A sample syllabus is included in Part IV (Useful Teaching Materials) of this manual.

2. **Distribute course requirements and a statement of the grading system.** Despite clear verbal explanations, some students do not understand or do not remember information which they are given about course requirements. Students are able to organize themselves more effectively if they are given a list of assignments, due dates, and test dates, in addition to a statement of how these will be used to determine grades.

3. **Relate and connect class sessions to one another.** Although a skill agenda clearly defines how the course is organized and shows how skills relate to one another, it is useful to reinforce this organization almost daily by tying together the previous class session with the current one and, at the end of a session, by giving a brief preview of the next class.

Collecting Student Data

It is useful to collect some basic information from each student during one of the first class sessions. In addition to such information as name, address, phone, and student ID number—useful for general record-keeping—you might ask each student to indicate the following:

1. curriculum and faculty advisor
2. year in college
3. current grade-point average, if any
4. whether he or she has taken a reading course earlier and, if so, where and when
5. other courses in which he or she is currently enrolled

These items will help you become familiar with each student and to adjust your content and approach to meet the particular needs of each class.

Pre-testing and Post-testing

If students have not taken a standardized reading test before entering the course, you might consider including a reading test as part of your first week's activities. A standardized reading test, most importantly, will give you an overview of the incoming student's ability. If the test reports a grade level or grade equivalency score, the results will give you an indication of the level at which the student can function adequately and will suggest types of materials appropriate to the student. Also, depending on the test used, it may indicate areas of strengths and weaknesses. To the student, the test results will demonstrate the need for the course and may motivate him or her to strive for improvement.

An alternative form of the same test at the end of the course can function as a post-test and, when compared to the pre-test, can indicate the improvement a student has made. Post-tests are particularly encouraging to students because they provide clear, measurable evidence for their improvement.

There is also a survey of students' attitudes toward reading on page 219 of this manual that may be helpful to give at the beginning of the course.

Class Session Format

Since some students have relatively short attention spans, it is important to include a variety of activities within each class session. Many students, for example, would have difficulty working on identifying main ideas for an entire class session of fifty to sixty minutes. It would be more effective to divide up the time by working with main ideas for twenty to thirty minutes and then switching to a Follow-Up activity on a skill previously taught, such as previewing, for the remaining time.

Skill Application and Transfer

The primary goal of this reading course is to teach students skills and techniques which they can apply to their academic courses. The skill-application exercises contained in the text are written to assist instructors in skill transfer. Instructors may also find the following suggestions useful:

1. Conduct a class discussion early in the semester about the utility of the skills and the importance of using them as they are learned. You might jokingly ask students if, while walking down the street, they have ever been stopped by a person and asked to explain how to preview, or whether they expect that to occur. This line of questioning demonstrates to the students that the skill is of no real value, except to themselves, and that it must be used in order to be valuable.

2. Discuss and review repeatedly the application of skills to the various disciplines. Utilize the readings from the college texts to provide students ample practice in making this skill transfer to as many different disciplines as possible. Assign students who are having difficulty in one area, additional practice utilizing the numerous readings provided for each discipline.

3. Informally spot-check the students and observe their reading behaviors in order to determine if they are using the skills taught. Check to see whether students are with their pencils in their hands, marking difficult vocabulary, annotating, or

reviewing after they read. Or, as you ask students to read a particular assignment and they begin reading, observe how many students preview the material before reading it.

Additional Practice

For additional practice, have students use the CD-ROM <u>Reading Road Trip</u>. Students can explore more exercises in the following categories:
- Memorization and Concentration
- Critical Thinking
- Vocabulary Patterns of Organization
- Note-Taking and Textbook Highlighting
- Reading Textbooks
- Outlining and Summarizing
- Test-Taking
- Inferences
- Purpose and Tone
- Graphics and Visual Aids
- Reading Rate

Part I: Handbook

"Art is communication, and if there is no communication it is as though the work had been stillborn. The reader, viewer, listener usually grossly underestimates his importance. If the reader cannot create a book along with the writer, the book will never come to life. Creative involvement: that's the basic difference between reading and watching TV. In watching TV we are passive, sponges; we do nothing. In reading we must become creators. . . .The author and the reader 'know' each other; they meet on the bridge of words."—Madeleine L'Engle

Active Learning

Introduction

- Show the following Hopi proverb to one student: "He who tells the stories rules the world." Ask the student to whisper the proverb to the student behind him or her. Continue this version of the old "Telephone" game until the message reaches the last student, who will then announce what the quote was. This demonstrates to the students the importance of being active, of paying attention, of attending class, and of constantly checking if he or she has accurately comprehended. Many students, if they are unclear about a concept, will simply wait and passively let someone else try to fix their learning problem.
- A good activity for the first day of class is to have the class brainstorm the attributes of a college student who excels in academics. Write these attributes on the board as you receive input from each student. Be sure that someone records the ideas, so you can provide a sheet of the characteristics that define a good student.
- In the interest of fairness, have students brainstorm the traits of a good teacher.

Input

- Discuss the information on active learning in the textbook. You may also want to mention the *Seven Habits of Highly Effective People* by Stephen Covey (Simon & Schuster, 1990) and explain that active learners are in tune, focused, and proactive.
- Ask students to create a visual representation or mnemonic device to help themselves remember these success traits. Explain that they should practice reciting these traits as they will come in handy during an interview.
- Discuss the textbook examples of active and passive readers. Compare your students' list of attributes that describes an excellent student with the characteristics that define an active reader.
- Make a transparency of the handout on the following page and have the students decide whether the speaker is an active or passive learner. (Afterward, assign students to go to the VARK Active Learning site and take the VARK Inventory to determine their learning style and strategies that facilitate how they learn: **www.vark-learn.com**).

Active or Passive Student?

- "I always look over my notes before and after each class."

- " I try to make sure I ask a question or answer a question during each class. That way I stay focused, and the instructor remembers me."

- "I go to most of my classes, but I always just listen. I get too distracted when I take notes."

- "If an assignment is given, I read it over once from the beginning in case the instructor asks if we did the homework."

- "I read an assignment once, and then I use some study strategies as a Follow-Up, especially if it's a tough course."

- "I study my lecture notes on Sunday night. I'll do the reading assignments if I get a chance."

- "I'm an auditory learner, so I make a tape of the lecture, and then I add to my notes when I listen to the tape again later."

- "Since I'm visual and kinesthetic, I use colored highlighters for main ideas and key details to memorize. I make flash cards, punch a hole in them, secure them with a ring, and flip through them when I'm in traffic or waiting in a doctor's office."

- "I don't really know what I want to do with my life, but I've met some great people here, and we usually get together at the pub on Thursday and Friday nights. We always intend to discuss a course, but . . ."

Previewing

Introduction

- Show the students a compass, a map, and an architect's blueprints. What do they have in common? Explain that previewing makes us more active, more in control, more focused. Previewing also helps us create a plan. Talk with students about the experience of reading a page and drawing a complete blank once the book is closed. This is a common problem. Explain that just as carpenters must build a frame to provide structure for a house, so must students create a framework for information if they are to remember it.
- Ask the students what an active learner might preview before reading a selection or assignment and list their answers on the board as they brainstorm.
- Read aloud an advertisement for a film or book and ask the students what they know about the material. What predictions can they make?

Input

- Have the students read the text discussion on the nine items for previewing. Then have them close their books and brainstorm what they can recall. On the board create a conceptual map of what they remember. Then have them open the text and compare their answers.

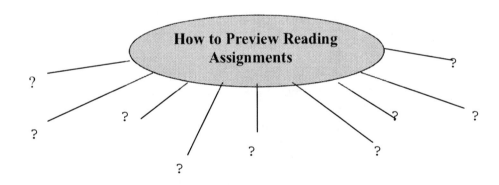

- Consider introducing some of the strategies in chapter 7, "Organizing Ideas," which discuss outlining, mapping, and process diagrams.
- As students to create an example of each method of organization in their notes along with a brief explanation of when they should be used. How do these compare to the framework mentioned at the beginning of the lesson?

Chapter 2: Vocabulary Building

"A wise man hears one word and remembers two."—Yiddish Proverb

Context Clues

Introduction

- Remind students that they are learning strategies to become active learners. On the board write the word *tantamount* and ask for ideas about what it means. Next, write the following sentence: According to Father Anthony, a Russian Orthodox priest, "To say 'I love you' is *tantamount* to saying 'you shall live forever.'" Explain to students that if they do not understand the word *tantamount*, they can mentally substitute it with a blank space wherein they can insert a familiar word that seems to work. In this way, they can make an intelligent guess at the meaning of the unknown word. (They will guess *equal, equivalent, the same as*—any of which is acceptable.)

- Next, write the word *moiety* and ask for suggestions. It's a tough one, but if you provide some clues, they will guess the meaning. Tell them the word appears in *The Adventures of Tom Sawyer* when Tom and Becky have become lost in the cave. When Becky becomes exasperated, crying that she is hungry, Tom reveals some cake he has saved. Twain wrote, "Tom divided the cake and Becky ate with good appetite, while Tom nibbled at his *moiety*." (They will guess *morsel, piece, slice, sliver, half, portion*—any of which is acceptable.)

- Then explain that with more than 600,000 words in the English language, and with the specialized vocabulary which they will encounter in subsequent college classes, students need a strong vocabulary. Also, with the latest trend for employers to give job candidates the *Prediction Indicator*, an inventory containing a comprehensive, two-sided list of adjectives on which they are to indicate words that describe themselves and words that describe the job for which they are applying, students need strategies to enhance their vocabulary. Therefore, to increase their vocabulary, active learners must become adept at identifying and applying **context clues**.

- An alternate introduction is to ask students to write a paragraph describing their favorite place. Then add, "Oh, by the way, you are not allowed to use the letter *t* anywhere in your essay." Then add, "Oh, by the way, you have only six minutes." When the students have completed writing during the six minutes, ask if anyone wants to share his or her description. Some may be eager to show off, but most students will agree the task was difficult. Explain that working with a weak vocabulary without some strategies to improve their knowledge of words may be tantamount to writing essays without being allowed to use the letter *t*.

18

Input

- Conclude the introduction with a conceptual map on the board of the context clues introduced in chapter 2: Vocabulary Building, and indicate the clue words they may encounter with each clue. (See the example below.)

- Kinesthetic learners will benefit from an activity with some movement. Create a list of words and definitions. Try to use words they will encounter in other disciplines, vocabulary words from their readings, or words you have discovered in your own reading. See the handout on pages 21-23. Make laminated cards with the word in one color and the definition in another color. Provide a transparency or handout of the list of sentences for each, requiring students to apply the context clues to discern the meaning of each italicized word. Put magnets on the back of the cards and have students match the definition you have given them to the magnetized card you have on the board. (You can purchase magnet strips at craft or office-supply stores.)

- Use the **guided note-taking handout** on the next page. Have the students review the clues you introduced earlier. Students will write in their answers as they are discussed in class, not independently.

Context Clues Conceptual Map

- This is an overview of the section on context clues. To give the students a view of the big picture, write the following conceptual map on the board and ask students for suggestions of clue words they might encounter with each category.

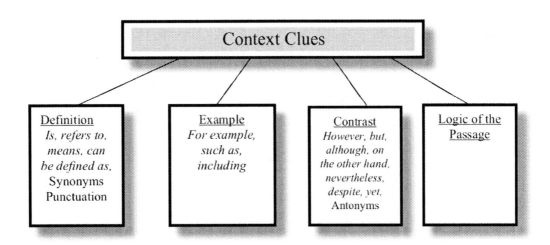

Context Clues

• Definition	(This clue includes signal words such as *is, refers to, means*; punctuation setting off synonyms, or brief definitions) *To become autonomous, or independent, is the goal of college students who aspire for academic success.* *Autonomous* means _____.
• Example	(Instead of synonyms or definitions, the author offers lists of words that share a common attribute.) *Novels by authors such as Stephen King, Dean Koontz, and V.C. Andrews frequently have sinister moods.* *Sinister means* _____.
• Contrast	(This clue includes transition words such as *however, on the other hand, despite, yet, nevertheless, conversely, contrarily, but, albeit, whereas, on the contrary, in contrast.*) *George could turn a simple "Hello" into a 30-minute story; however, his laconic brother John simply gave a short "Hi" and continued with his work.* *Laconic* means _____.
• Passage Logic	(Look for clues beyond the unknown word by pretending it is a blank.) *The new band students made such a cacophonous sound that I had to cover my ears.* *Cacophonous* means _____.

- Using the list of words and their definitions, print the words on one color of paper and the definitions on white. Put magnetic strips on the back of each word and definition. Give each student a word and put the definition on the board. Then have students refer to the sentences—either as a handout or as a transparency you have prepared. Students will deduce the meanings of each using context clues and will match their word to the definition. If you do this as a group, you can have students point out context clues that helped them discover the meaning.

Vocabulary Word	Definition
Abstemious	moderate in eating and drinking
Assuage	to calm; to relieve
Auspicious	favorable
Cacophony	a harsh, unpleasant sound
Condone	to pardon; to forgive
Cryptic	secret; hidden
Disparage	to demoralize; lower the spirits
Extraneous	unnecessary; not essential
Innate	natural; inborn
Relegate	to assign to an inferior position
Scrupulous	honest; upright; careful in detail
Subjugate	to conquer
Truculent	cruel; savage
Vacillate	to waver; to sway
Vilify	to malign; to condemn openly

Using Context Clues

1. The prosecutor objected that the witness's testimony was not relevant to the case, and the judge agreed, saying that the information was *extraneous* and unnecessary.

   Extraneous means_____

2. His encounter with the savvy stockbroker proved *auspicious* when he acted on the tip and tripled his investment within the month.

   Auspicious means_____

3. All humans have an *innate* need for social interaction at times, whether they are introverts or extroverts.

   Innate means_____

4. The *cacophony* generated by the street noises—blaring radio, distant sirens, and unchecked car mufflers—forced the student to seek quiet study at the library.

   Cacophony means_____

5. Because of his honesty, the *scrupulous* accountant was in great demand during tax season.

   Scrupulous means_____

6. Following the debacle of allowing his ship to drift into the path of an approaching vessel, the captain was relieved of his command and *relegated* to whale-watching in the North Sea.

   Relegated means_____

7. After a series of poor judgments and serious personal indiscretions, the politician was *vilified* by angry constituents, by embarrassed colleagues, and by ruthless members of the press who relished the opportunity to subject him to public ridicule.

   Vilified means_____

8. Though he enjoyed socializing at parties, the judge was always careful to be moderate in his eating and *abstemious* in his drinking of alcohol.

   Abstemious means_____

9. Her *truculent* behavior frequently alienated friends and colleagues, who found her manners offensive, abrasive, and constantly annoying.

   Truculent means_____

10. During the parenting classes, expectant mothers and fathers learn positive strategies to *assuage* a crying baby.

    Assuage means_____

11. Though he expected candidness from his best friend, he realized his own behavior had become *cryptic* and secret. In fact, he frequently excluded everyone from his activities and remained pensively silent about his thoughts.

    Cryptic means_____

12. Whenever he tried to get the nerve to propose marriage, Sam would suddenly *vacillate* between a longing to spend the rest of his life with his girlfriend and a compelling desire to remain unattached.

    Vacillate means_____

13. They could not *condone* the flagrant cheating, which was obvious to any observer; consequently, the student was identified and eventually dismissed from the university.

    Condone means_____

14. Owen always felt demoralized when his uncle *disparaged* his accomplishments, belittling the academic successes he achieved instead of offering him some well-deserved acclaim.

    Disparage means_____

15. After only seven minutes in the ring, the wrestler was able to *subjugate* his opponent and emerge from the ring as the champion.

    Subjugate means_____

Word Parts

Introduction

- In his book, *The Big Picture*, Dr. Benjamin Carson, chief of pediatric neurosurgery at Johns Hopkins Hospital, explains an inspired procedure for separating *craniopagus* twins. In order to diminish the possibility of *hemorrhaging*, he performed the surgery with the twins in a *hypothermal* state. Immediately following the surgery, Dr. Carson watched the twins' vital signs to determine their *prognosis.* (Carson, *The Big Picture,* Zondervan Publishing House, 1999, pp. 11-12)

- As you are sharing this information, write the words on the board and ask students if they can determine the definitions using context clues. They may be able to do this, but you can add that, with a little knowledge of some Greek and Latin, they would be more proficient if context clues are not available. (Explain the roots: *cranio*=helmet; *pagus*=fixed; *hemo*=blood; *hypo*=below; *therm*=heat; *pro*=forward; *gnosis*=to know.)

- Next, tell the students that active learners aspire to be *autonomous,* or independent, rather than want to rely on others to solve their academic challenges. Although you used a synonym as a definition clue in that sentence, tell them that *auto-* means "self." Consequently, with that information, they could discern that an autonomous person is self-sufficient.

Input

- After you give students an brief overview of the function and some examples of **prefixes**, **roots**, and **suffixes** and how learning word parts can enhance their lives, provide more detailed information following the text section for the students using the inductive method on the chart designed for Cornell Notes. Through guided note-taking and using some critical reading, they will determine the definitions of the word parts as you provide examples of words with those prefixes, roots, and suffixes.

- With each category, point out how learning word parts, or word analysis, will help them. For instance, when teaching prefixes, you can tell the poor spellers that learning why we spell words a certain way will help them remember, and frequently the rationale for some spellings is the use of word parts. For example, *mis* + spell= misspell, meaning *wrong* + *spell*; *dis* + sect = dissect, meaning *separated from* + *sections.*

- Other examples are words with negative prefixes. For instance, you may add *ir-* to words beginning with *r*, as in *irresponsible; irregular; irreverent.* Or you may add *im-* to words that begin with *m* or *p*, as in *impossible; immature; immaterial; imperfect.* Finally, you might add *il* to words that begin with the letter *l*, as in *illegal; illegible.* When discussing word parts, remind students that some have multiple meanings. While *im* often negates a word, an *impassioned* speech is full of enthusiasm and fervor. And while *in* can mean *not*, something that is *invaluable*—like your great-grandfather's gold pocket watch—is irreplaceable, very valuable. (Again, using context clues, when available, can be helpful.)

Word Parts: Guided Note-Taking (Fill in the blanks.)

Prefixes

Word Part	Definition	Examples
(Negative Prefixes)		
un, non		unkind, unimportant, unreal nonfat, nonstop, nonfiction
a		amoral, apolitical, atypical
anti		antiwar, antiballistic, antithesis
contra, contro		contradict, contraband, controversy
in, im, il, ir		ineffective, immoral, illegible, irresponsible
dis		disagree, disingenuous
mis		misspell, misinterpret, misogynist, miscreant
mal		malicious, malinger, malign, malevolent, malfeasance
pseudo		pseudonym, pseudoscience, pseudopod
(Number/Amount Prefixes)		
auto		automobile, autograph, autonomy, autocracy
mono/uni		monopoly, monotone, union, unify, unicycle
bi/di/du		bicycle, dilemma, duet
tri		tripod, tricycle, triumverate
quad/quart		quadrant, quarter
pent		pentagon, pentarchy
deci		decade, decathlon
cent		century, centurion, centennial
milli/kilo		million, millimeter, kilocalorie, kilometer
micro		microscope, microbiology
multi/poly		multiply, multitude, polygamy, polychromatic
semi/hemi		semisweet, hemisphere
equi		equity, equivalent

Prefixes (continued)

Word Part	Definition	Examples
(Direction, Location, Placement Prefixes)		
ab		absent
ad		advent, adhesive
ante/pre		anterior, anteroom prefix, pretest
circum/peri		circumference, circumspect, circumnavigate, perimeter
com/col/con		compile, commemorate compliant, collaborate, collide, convene, connect
de		depart, detour, delete
dia		diameter, dialog, diaphragm
dis		disaster, dismiss, disperse
ex/extra		ex-wife, exhale, extraterrestrial
hyper		hypertension, hyperactive, hyperglycemia
hypo		hypotension, hypodermic, hypoglycemia, hypothermia
inter		interrupt, interpersonal, intermittent, intervene
intro/intra		introduction, intravenous
post		postpone, postpartum, postdate
re		revitalize, retort, review
retro		retrospect, retroactive
sub		subjugate, submarine, subsequent
super		supervise, supersede, supercharge
tele		telescope, telepathy
trans		transcend, transition

Roots

Word Part	Definition	Example
ann, enn		annual, perennial, millennium
arch		archetype, monarch
aud, audit		auditory, auditorium, audition
aster, astro		asterisk, disaster, astronomy
bene		benediction, benefit, benevolent
biblio		bibliography, bibliophile
bio		biology, biography
cap		captive, captivate, capitulation
chron		synchronize, chronicle
chrom		monochrome, chromosome
claim, clam		exclaim, proclaim, exclamatory
corp		corporation, corpse, corpulent
cor, cour		corsage, courage, coronary
cred		credible, credulous, incredible, incredulous
cycl, cyclo		cyclical, cyclone
dict, dic		predict, dictate, contradiction
duc, duct		conduct, induct, deduce
fact, fac		factory, manufacture, malefactor, benefactor
fin		finite, infinite, finale, finial
flex, flect		reflex, reflection, inflection, deflect
forc, fort		fortify, enforce, reinforcement
geo		geography, geology, geocentric
graph		autograph, monograph
hum		humanity, humble

log, logo, logy		microbiology, zoology
loqu		loquacious, soliloquy
mater, matri		maternal, matriarch
mit, miss		emit, mission, permission
mort, mor		mortify, moribund, morgue, mortuary
pater, patri		paternal, paternity, patronymic, patriot
path		empathy, pathetic, apathy
pend		dependent, suspend, pendulum, pendant
phil		philosophy, Philadelphia, videophile, philanthropist
phob		phobia, claustrophobia
phono		phonetic, telephone
photo		photography, photosynthesis
pop		populist, popular, populace
port		export, transport, portable
psych, psycho		psychology, psychic
rect		rectify, direct, erect
scop		telescope, microscope
scrib, script		describe, ascribe, prescription, description
sen, sent		sentient, sensitive
spec, spic, spect		spectator, retrospect, inspect
tend, tent, tens		tendency, intention, tension
terri, terre		territory, terrace, terrain, extra-terrestrial
theo		atheist, theology, theocracy
ven, vent		convene, circumvent, intervene, ventilation
vis, vid		envision, video, visual
voc		vocation, vocal, avocation

Suffixes

Word Part	Definition	Part of Speech	Example
able	able to, having qualities of,		comparable
ance	quality or state of being		assistance
ation	act of, condition, result		revelation
ence	quality or state of being		persistence
ible	able to, having qualities of		compatible
ion	result, condition		reaction
ity	state or condition; character		integrity
ive	relating to; having the quality of		pensive
ment	result; means; process; state or condition		agreement
ness	state, quality		openness
ous	full of; having, characterized by		loquacious
ty	quality or condition		loyalty
y	quality or condition		scary
an	one who		Egyptian
ant	one who		participant
ee	one who		designee
eer	one who		engineer
ent	one who		resident
er, or	one who		reader, author
ist	one who		activist
al	like or suitable; act or process of		autumnal
ship	quality; condition; ability		friendship
hood	state of being; quality; condition		statehood
ward	in the direction of		homeward

- Make a set of laminated, magnetized cards for students to match definitions to word parts that you have written on the board. Make each category (prefix, root, suffix) a different color, so students can differentiate, and you can discuss words containing those parts as you consider their choices that they indicated on the board.

- This second practice activity on the next page should be presented in the form of a transparency. Tell students that some test questions may come from this review. Cover each question with a small Post-It and unveil a question as you move from one student to the next. If a student cannot answer, he or she should be allowed to call on a "lifeline" since the purpose is to discover what they know. (Be sure to give prizes: Smarties, Dum-Dums, and sugar-free candy are popular items, especially if you pass them around while the game is in progress and make sure everyone is a winner.)

Word Analysis Trivia

Prefix	Prefix	Root	Root	Root	Suffix
Define *anti.*	Define *peri.*	Define *cred.*	Define *vis.*	Define *voc.*	Define *or.*
A *misanthrope* is someone who does good or bad	If you *circumvent* a problem, you…	A *graphologist* probably analyzes…	Someone who has *apathy* is without…	A *subterranean* cave is located where?	A suffix changes the meaning of a word as well as this.
The *anterior* of the pig you dissect in biology is in the...	If you *contradict* your thesis, you…	Literally, if you *mortify* someone, you embarrass them to…	A *chronometer* measures. . .	A *benefactor* is someone who…	Words ending with *-tion, -er,* and *-or* are probably what part of speech?
If you *intercede* in negotiations, what do you do?	A *polytheistic* religion worships…	If you are suffering from *photophobia,* you…	At one time people believed in a *geocentric* universe, which meant…	If we *incorporate* our ideas, we put them into one…	Words ending in *–fy, -ate,* and *-ize* are probably what part of speech?

Chapter 3: Thesis, Main Ideas, Supporting Details, and Transitions

"A good reader is one who has imagination, memory, a dictionary, and some artistic sense." –Vladimir Nabokov

General and Specific

Introduction

- Read aloud (or reproduce as a transparency) the lines from the conversation between the brother and sister, Rebecca and George, in *Our Town* by Thornton Wilder. See the handout on page 33 of the manual. In this passage Rebecca explains about the letter from the minister to Jane Crofut, and it is an example of moving from narrow to broad, from very specific to more general.
- Begin this chapter by explaining to the students about the difference in the terms **general** and **specific** or **broad** and **narrow**. These terms will help the students progress from an understanding of the main concept, or thesis, to a recognition of the supporting details.
- Visuals are important when introducing this concept. For instance, nesting cups or nesting dolls with four sections can show how items in a paragraph develop from the general (as in the all-encompassing outer cup that represents the thesis) to the most specific (the tiny inner cup that represents the minor, supporting details).
- Another visual that helps is a drawing of concentric circles on the chalkboard. Label the outer one as the thesis (or topic), the next as the topic sentence, the next as the major detail, and the last one as a minor detail. An example is provided on page 34.
- A third way of introducing the concepts of general and specific is to create a ladder on the chalkboard. (See the example on page 35.) Demonstrate one example, and then have the students offer suggestions for a second or third. Note that the first item on the top step is the most general. To identify the next noun, ask, "What kind?" or "Which one?" Explain to the students that with each step down, the category gets smaller and smaller.
- Point out that when we are more specific in our writing or speaking, then the reader or hearer "sees the same movie" in his or her head as we do. Consequently, we more accurately convey our message.
- Make a transparency of the table on page 36 to show students the difference in general and specific concepts.

General and Specific

(from *Our Town* by Thornton Wilder)

Rebecca: I never told you about the letter Jane Crofut got from her minister when she was sick. He wrote Jane a letter and on the envelope the address was like this: It said, Jane Crofut; The Crofut Farm; Grover's Corners; Sutton County, New Hampshire; of America

George: What's funny about that?

Rebecca: But listen, it's not finished: the of America; Continent of North America; Western Hemisphere; the Earth; the Solar System; the Universe; the Mind of God—that's what it said on the envelope.

George: What do you know!

Rebecca: And the postman brought it just the same.

Visual Representations of Paragraph Structure

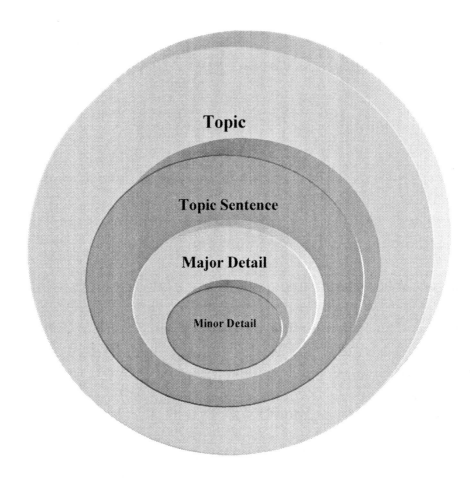

Give students a blank sheet of paper and ask them to create their own visual concepts of main ideas and supporting details. Invite them to display their work and explain the components. Some ideas to help them get started are as follows:

Chocolate chip cookie
Woman's purse
Train
House
Shopping mall
Baseball Team
Pizza

General to Specific

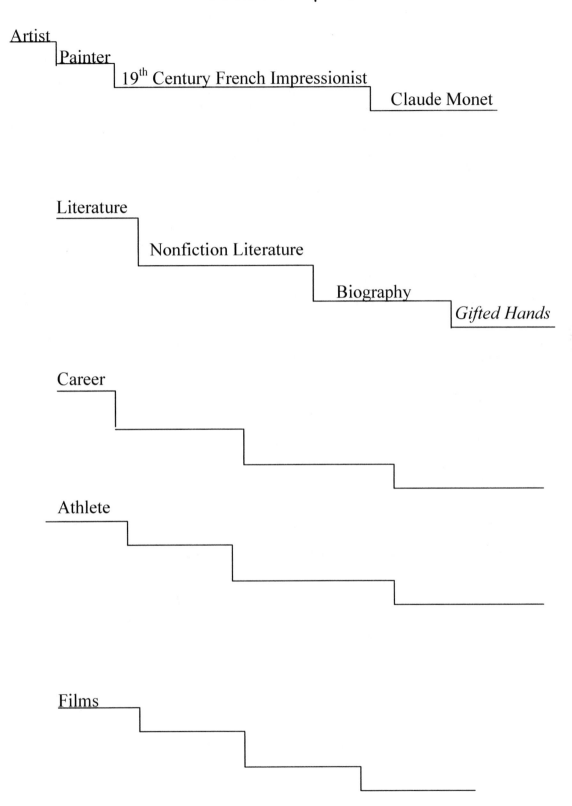

The Difference Between General and Specific Ideas

General	Specific
❖ Thesis (or Topic)	❖ Major Details
❖ Topic Sentence	❖ Minor Details
❖ Thesis Statement	❖ Bring the General into Focus
❖ Broad	❖ Narrow
❖ Encompass Much	❖ Clarify
❖ Conclude	❖ Explain
❖ Act as a Springboard	❖ Convince
❖ Expand Meaning	❖ Support
❖ May Be Misinterpreted	❖ Restrict Interpretations
❖ Distill	❖ Crystallize
❖ Summarize	❖ Specify

Main Idea: An Overview

Terms	Explanation
Thesis or Topic	General Subject
Main Idea	Primary point about the thesis. It may be stated or implied.
Topic Sentence	States the topic and primary point about that topic in a paragraph. (It may appear anywhere in the paragraph.)
Thesis Statement	the essay, and will appear in the introductory States the topic and primary point about paragraph.
Major Details	Support the main idea
Minor Details	Support the major details. They are not essential to the main idea, but help embellish the major details.
Transition words	These often introduce the supporting details. Occasionally, they can introduce a topic sentence or a thesis statement. Examples include: First, second , next, finally, therefore, as a result, furthermore, in addition, likewise, whereas, on the contrary, however, on the other hand, albeit, whereas, but, despite, nevertheless.

*(Cover the answers, which are in small, underlined print.)

Input

- One of the most difficult things for students is to move from a topic or thesis to a **topic sentence** or **thesis statement**. Frequently, students are not able to discern a fragment from a complete sentence. The following activity is designed to give them practice:

On index cards, write the following topics. Depending on the number of students in the class, make at least two copies of the topics below so that each student will be given a card and will have a partner in the class.

Special privileges which college athletes receive
Things to look for when buying a used car
How to prepare for a job interview
Hot careers of the new millennium
Attributes of an active learner
Steps to previewing a reading assignment
The three most important films of the past 25 years
Qualities of my favorite restaurant
Effective advertisements on TV
Examples of animal emotions
Ways to end a relationship
Characteristics of a good leader
The three most important inventions of the past 50 years

After giving each student a card, model the activity by writing a conceptual map on the board:

Steps to follow for making a shot in basketball

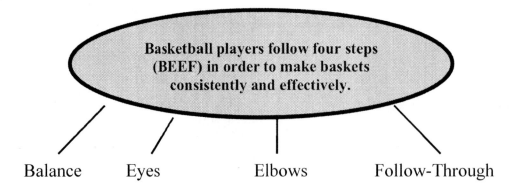

- Explain how you took the general topic, or thesis, and expanded it into a complete sentence to create a topic sentence in a paragraph. The steps raying out from the oval serve as supporting details that clarify, expand, and explain.

- Next, pair each student with the classmate who has the same thesis. Ask them to collaborate and create a logical topic sentence, which would be an expansion of the thesis. Again, point out that the thesis (topic) could sound like a title, but it should *not* be the topic sentence. After you have circulated the room to check on the students' wording and accuracy of the topic sentence, allow the students to establish the supporting details. Explain that writers like to do things in threes, so they must have at least three supporting details. However, some topics (such as "Ways to End a Relationship") will obviously have more. Again, circulate the room and check on the logic of the supporting details. (Point out that only the topic sentence needs to be a complete sentence.) Finally, have the students go to the board and share their conceptual maps.(If some students are in a developmental writing course, this exercise will be beneficial and you may suggest that they consider some of these topics for subsequent writing assignments.)

- To facilitate students' ability to recognize topic sentences, explain the possible locations discussed in the chapter (first, middle, last, as well as first and last). Next, introduce some of the operative words that writers of college texts may use as a springboard to discuss supporting details. Make a transparency of the visual on the next page and list a variety of words that may indicate a topic sentence. Point out that while writers are not limited to the words on this list, these are the kinds of words that students will frequently encounter in textbook reading.

- For practice, make transparencies of the visuals on pages 41-43.

Key Words for Locating and Writing Topic Sentences:

Phases; Series; Results; Consequences; Ways; Reasons;

Contributions; Methods; Kinds; Causes; Outcomes;

Features; Steps; Factors; Types; Traits; Effects;

Aspects; Categories; Examples; Attributes;

Levels; Characteristics; Conclusions;

Elements; Stages; Instances;

Processes; Techniques;

Routines

Identifying Main Idea: Indicate the thesis (general subject), main idea statement, and three specific supporting details.

A. High-tech equipment increases the performance of athletes.

B. How high-tech equipment affects athletes' performance in sports.

C. Ultra-aerodynamic bicycles result in faster times for cyclists.

D. New swimsuit designs are modeled after sharkskin and enhance speed.

E. Carbon-fiber boats and oars can improve rowing performance.

Identifying Main Idea: Indicate the thesis (topic), main idea statement, and two supporting details.

A. *Folk* sports consisted of foot-racing and fist fighting—activities that were consistent with a commoner's daily life.

B. Two historical categories of sport.

C. Prior to the Industrial Revolution, sport could be divided into two categories: *elite* and *folk*.

D. *Elite* sports such as polo, hunting, and riding were frequently a part of the daily leisure of the upper class.

Identifying Main Idea: Locate the thesis (topic), main idea statement, and three supporting details.

A. Many famous buildings share a basic construction element: the arch.

B. The Hoover Dam is a sideways arch that uses water as the compression force.

C. G. Eiffel, designer of the famous tower, applied the concept of the arch to his structure.

D. Ancient Romans built bridges, aqueducts, and domes using the arch.

E. The ubiquitous arch.

Implied Main Idea

- Remind students that not all paragraphs contain a topic sentence (or a stated main idea). Some writers require the reader to **infer** (conclude or reason) a main idea, which is **implied** (suggested or hinted). First show the map below and have the class decide what the main idea is. Then explain that the writer could have presented the details without a clearly stated main idea sentence, and the reader could still conclude the main idea.

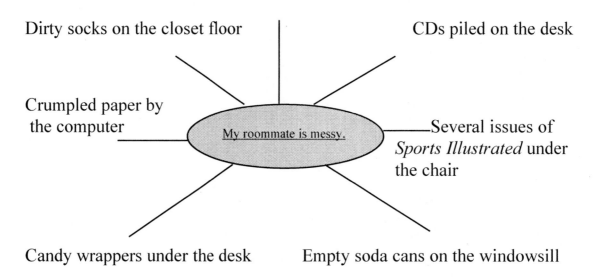

- Remind the students to identify the topic by asking, "What is the one thing the author might discuss?"
- Have them look at each detail and decide what larger idea each detail explains.
- Have them express the main idea in their own words: "My roommate is messy."

Supporting Details

- Following your lectures on thesis and main idea, use repetition to drill students on their understanding. Anthony Robbins states, "Repetition is the mother of mastery." Nowhere is mastery more critical than in identifying thesis and main idea statements. Be sure students are confident in their understanding of these concepts by providing opportunities for reinforcement.
- Choose any appropriate paragraph to put on an overhead. Ask the students to read the paragraph for understanding. Then ask them to reread it a second time, underlining the main idea sentence and highlighting any signal words that denote either the main idea or details. Explain that many students stop after reading an assignment just one time and assume they have "studied." In fact, they are only one-fourth of the way finished. (They will probably not do well on exams if they stop at this point.) They need to take the next step, which involves thinking about the information and noting the main ideas and the supporting details. (Now they are beginning to build a framework for knowledge.) They are still only half-way finished, however. Next, provide students with large strips of cardboard (old folders work well for this) which have the topic, main idea sentence, and details on separate pieces that have magnets on the back. Pass the pieces around to class members, and ask them to reconstruct the paragraph in outline form on the board. Then gather up the strips and ask other students to reconstruct the same paragraph, but this time help them create a map for the visual learners, drawing circles or squares around the information and lines to show how they are linked. Next, ask students to do this in their notes as an example. Now they are three-fourths of the way finished. (They are applying bricks and mortar to their framework.) Finally, explain that the very last step involves memorizing the information. This won't be difficult because they have built a solid framework. Only then have they taken the steps necessary for studying college subjects. Once they have built a solid framework of knowledge, they will see the reward in "solid" grades on their tests.
- Use an inductive approach to further explain supporting details. Since you have laid the foundation with an explanation of the terms *general* and *specific*, this will be an easy transition. Put the following conceptual map on the board or make a transparency and have the students determine the thesis and topic sentence that the details support.

Can you solve this puzzle?

Thesis: (<u>What do these details suggest? What might the topic or general idea be?</u>)

Helps maintain weight

Improves memory

Strengthens bones

Elevates mood — ? — Enhances appearance

Strengthens bones — Strengthens muscles

Improves cardiovascular system

What are the details? _____

What do the details have in common? _____

What topic is suggested by the details? _____

How could you create a general sentence that summarizes these details? ____

(Students should determine that the thesis is "The Benefits of Exercise" and the main idea statement will be "Exercise benefits the body in several ways.")

- Using the index cards with topics that the students previously considered when changing topics to topic sentences, have groups of students organize an outline or conceptual map that would be a prewriting activity for paragraph or thesis writing. Give groups of three or four students one of the cards, markers, and chart paper. Have them organize supporting details (major and minor) that they would use in a paragraph or essay for that topic/topic sentence/thesis statement. Assign a *leader* who acts as a facilitator and selects a *note-taker,* someone who will write the group members' ideas as they brainstorm; an *artist,* someone who puts the ideas on the chart paper; and a *presenter,* someone who will share with the class the results of the activity. If you have more than four in the group, be sure everyone has a job by asking the leader to assign two people as artists, note-takers, and/or presenters. (This activity, which appeals to students with all learning styles, is even more successful if you bring in a camera and take pictures of the students in their groups. Then, as a Follow-Up, have the group come to the front of the room and present their chart to the class.)

Transitions

- At this point, explain that authors use transition words to signal supporting details. Since *trans* mean *change* and *across,* these words flag a change or a move across from one supporting detail to another. While transition words can introduce a supporting detail, they do not always, so make that clear. Otherwise students will just look for the transitions. (At this point, you may want to explain that transitions can occasionally introduce a topic sentence or thesis statement. For instance, an author can "hook" the reader with a statement, then offer a contrast transition word to shift to the real focus of the paragraph or essay. Use the example below:

Many people believe college freshmen lead lives filled with carefree activities and little stress. *However,* first-year students must contend with a myriad of difficulties: the high cost of tuition and living expenses; the need to develop effective study strategies to tackle demanding courses; and the opportunity to acquaint themselves with people with diverse backgrounds and different personal philosophies.

Use the following handout as a guided note-taking activity to help students mentally organize different kinds of transitions and their function:

TRANSITIONS

Directions: Fill in the blanks using the information from your textbook.

Types of Transitions	Example	Function
	First, second, third, next, then, during, meanwhile, finally	The author arranges ideas in the order in which they happened. Order is then critical.
Example		An example will follow.
Enumeration		The author is marking or identifying each major point. (Sometimes these may be used to suggest order of importance.)
	Also, in addition, and, furthermore, another, moreover	The author is continuing with the same idea and is going to provide additional information.
Contrast		The author is switching to a different, opposite, or contrasting idea than previously discussed.
Comparison	*Like, likewise, similarly, in comparison, just as, as well*	
Cause-Effect		The writer will show a connection between two or more things, how one thing caused another, or how something happened as a result of something else.

Chapter 4: Organizational Patterns

"The events in our lives happen in a sequence in time, but in their significance to ourselves, they find their own order. . . the continuous thread of revelation."—Eudora Welty

Introduction

- Draw a circle on the board and explain that the Greeks believed the circle was the most perfect form. Consequently, writers often begin and end their works with a thread of similarity: a reference in the conclusion to something mentioned in the introduction—a word, a quotation, a concept.
- To help students with this idea of **form**, use an example from a current film—one you have already thought through—and explain how something at the beginning related to something at the end, usually to indicate a resolution of a conflict.
- Next, explain that writers deliberately follow a form, frequently to communicate with the reader in an organized way. Therefore, learning to recognize organizational patterns will help students:
    - focus their reading;
    - anticipate an author's thought development;
    - improve their own writing.
- Remind students of the analogy of building a framework of knowledge just as a carpenter builds a frame for a house. The reader must determine the framework or build a framework that will organize information in order to learn it. Knowledge of organizational patterns will provide a blueprint for the study required to master college courses.

Input

- Provide the following table as a guided note-taking activity for the chapter overview. Note that this table follows the same wording in the text on page 91: "Summing It Up: Patterns and Transitions." Ask students to fill in the blank spaces.
- Write the transition words in bold print on 4 by 6-inch index cards. Attach magnetic strips to the backs. Divide the board into ten categories and give each student two or three cards. Ask them to decide the category for each word and to place these in the appropriate box. Once students have completed the task, ask the class to determine if any changes need to be made. Note that some of the categories can use the same transitions. Do the same for the characteristics of each pattern. Repeat this exercise as a practice and drill activity throughout several lessons at the beginning or end of class.

Organizational Patterns

Pattern	Characteristics	Transitions and Signal Words
1. _____	Explains the meaning of a word or phrase; used in most introductory-level texts.	*Is, means, refers to, can be defined as, another term, also means*
2. Classification	Divides a topic into parts based on shared characteristics; used in many academic subjects.	
3. Order or Sequence	Describes the order or sequence in which something occurs. May be divided into several sub-categories: • Chronological Order • Process • Order of Importance • Spatial Order	
4. _____	Describes causes and results; describes a relationship between two or more actions, events, or occurrences; widely used in the sciences, technologies, and social sciences.	
5. _____	Discusses similarities and/or differences among ideas, theories, concepts, objects, or persons.	
6. Listing/Enumeration	Organizes lists of information: characteristics, features, parts, categories.	*The following, several, for instance, for example, one instance, one, another, also, too, in other words, first, second, (1,2,3), (a,b,c), most important, largest, least*
7. Statement and Clarification		*Clearly, evidently, obviously*
8. _____	Indicates that a condensed review of an idea or piece of writing will follow.	*In summary, in conclusion, in brief, to summarize, to sum up, in short, on the whole*
9. Generalization and Example	Provides examples that clarify a broad, general statement.	
10. Addition	Indicates that more information will follow.	

- Once students have an overview of the patterns, give them the opportunity to participate in some inductive, hands-on activities. For example, type various organizational patterns in one color of ink and font style, make enough copies for everyone in the class, laminate the copies, and cut them into strips. Next, do the same using a different color of ink for the function/characteristics. Finally, make a set in a third color and font style for the signal and transition words. You should have three strips per pattern. Scramble these and put them in an envelope. Have the students match pattern, characteristic, and transition/signal words. (This is best done in pairs. If you laminate the strips, you will be able to use them for subsequent classes and semesters.)

- In order to assist the students in applying this new information, offer them a second inductive activity. Print each of the following simple paragraphs (A,B,C,D) on different colors of paper. Laminate each set and cut the sentences, so that you have five strips per paragraph. Scramble each set and secure with a paper clip. Put all four sets in an envelope. (Make enough of these for all students to work independently.) Circulate around the room to check the order of the sentences. Remind them to use transition words as clues. When they have completed the activity, show the same sentences as a transparency and ask the students to identify transitions and signal words that served as clues. Underline these with a colored marker as they suggest the words.

- Using a transparency of the visual on page 54, have the students make a connection with the graphics and identify the organizational pattern of each picture.

- As a final review, ask students to fold a sheet of paper lengthwise into thirds, creasing the folds sharply. Then ask them to unfold it and fold again the other way into thirds. Once the paper is unfolded, they will have nine "windows." Instruct them to write the name of one of the organizational patterns in each box, with the last one added to the back. Now, have them circulate around the room and collect signatures from a different student for each box. In order to get the signature, however, they must be able to correctly explain the function of the pattern.

Windows

A

- Founded by the Greek philosopher Zeno, Stoicism stressed living a virtuous life in harmony with natural laws.

  Also, the philosophy promoted social unity.

  Third, Stoics, who believed in a divine power, viewed human desires as dangerous.

  As a result, self-discipline was highly revered.

B

- Mnemonics is a memory-enhancing strategy which active learners practice to help them remember lists.

  One traditional example is HOMES, a memory trick to remember the Great Lakes: Huron, Ontario, Michigan, Erie, and Superior.

  Another is the absurd phrase, "All snakes dig tunnels," which helps government students recall the list of specialized courts: appeals, small claims, divorce, and traffic.

  Yet another is SPA, which is used to help students remember the chronological order of Greek philosophy, since the letters signify "Socrates taught Plato, who taught Aristotle."

C

- Cognitive psychologists studying effective study strategies have discovered three major learning styles.
One predominant style is visual.
These visual learners use clues they can see and thus frequently doodle in their notes and use colored markers to highlight important concepts.
Another style is auditory.
Students who rely on listening to absorb information have found taping lectures and replaying them at various times of the day helpful.
In addition, these same learners find that reading aloud is very beneficial to their style.
Finally, a third style is kinesthetic.
A kinesthetic, or hands-on learner, needs movement to facilitate learning.
Consequently, they often need to walk around as they read particularly challenging chapters, or they could make flash cards to move and match concepts and definitions.

D

- Did you heard about the mysterious light in West Point, near a popular teen-age hangout?
The enigmatic glow has been attributed to phosphorous-filled swamp gases.
However, another theory, an urban legend, is that an ill-fated train brakeman roams the area in search of his head.
Like most urban legends, the story is actually a morality story with three goals.
First, it serves as a warning.
Second, it is related to social change.
And finally, it was created to instill guilt and fear.

Organizational Patterns

Is, refers to, can be defined as, means, consists of	*Classified as, is comprised of, is composed of, varieties, stages, groups*	*First, second, later, before, next, as soon as, during, meanwhile, when, until*
First, second, next, then, following, after that, last, finally	*Above, below, beside, next to, in front of, behind, inside, outside, nearby*	*Because, since, leads to, reason, produces, due to, consequently, therefore, results in, thus, hence*
Both, also, similarly, like, unlike, nevertheless, despite, yet, however, on the other hand	*1,2,3; a,b,c; first, second, third, next, finally*	*In fact, in other words, to clarify, evidently, obviously*

"Imagine where we'd be in physics if we hadn't inferred what's inside the atom."—Jaak Panksepp

Introduction

- Show the students a penny, a nickel, and a dime. Explain that you are going to tell them a riddle, and it is important for them to focus on all of the details. Say, "Bob's mother had three children. The first one she named Penny." (At this point, hold up the penny.) "The next one she named Nicky." (Show the nickel.) "The third one she named . . ." (Have the students guess the name of the third child as you show the dime.) At first students will guess names such as Dimetrius or Dimey. Praise them for their attempts, and encourage them to guess. Explain that you will tell the riddle again and stress that they need to focus on the details. Eventually, someone will guess "Bob."
- Write the words *imply* and *infer* on the board and explain that these are not interchangeable terms. Since *imply* means *to hint or suggest* and *infer* means *to conclude*, the former involves *sending* information and the latter involves *receiving* information.
- Next, point out the photograph of the firefighter and dog in the textbook and explain that we make inferences every day. Ask for some examples of inferences they make daily.

Input

- Then, put the conceptual map on page 56 on the board to give students an overview.
- Show the process diagram on page 57 to explain the steps to making inferences.
- Locate cartoons without captions that can be duplicated on overheads. (*The Far Side* cartoons are particularly good for this activity. Ask students to determine the meaning and humor of the cartoon. Challenge them to point out the details in the cartoon and ask them to keep these details in mind. The point of humor will be supported by the details.
- Next, divide students into small groups and give each group a cartoon picture that has no caption. Challenge each group to write a suitable caption and explain it to the class.

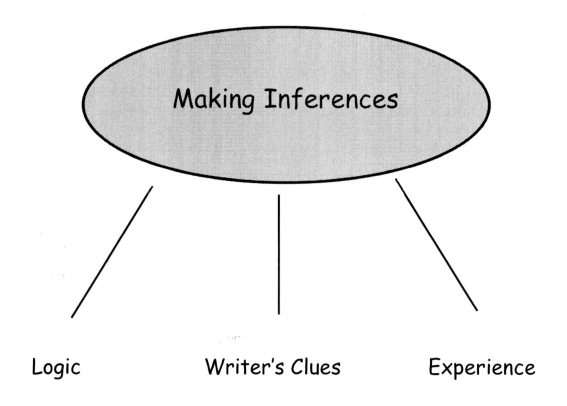

Logic   Writer's Clues   Experience

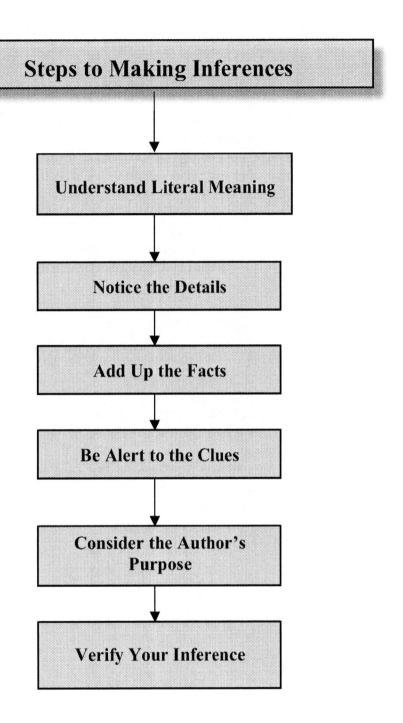

- Point out that literary allusions involve making inferences. A good example is the scene from the film *Air Force One* in which the President's plane has been highjacked with him on board. In a secret phone conversation with his Vice-President, the Commander-in-Chief refuses to allow his government to negotiate with the terrorists. "But why, Mr. President?" He responds, "If you give a mouse a cookie." Show the children's book by the same name. It is very short, and you can even read it aloud. Then ask the students to deduce, from the facts, their logic, and their own experience, what he means. (There are other allusions to which the students will relate. Another example is the implication in the film *The Matrix* when a character draws a parallel with Kansas after the tornado in *The Wizard of Oz,* and says, "Kansas has gone bye-bye" in order to explain how Earth has changed.) Or you can discuss inferences which advertisers and campaigning politicians encourage us to make. Probably the front page of any newspaper will provide proof that we must make inferences every day. Therefore, learning to make accurate inferences can actually enhance the quality of our lives.

- An interesting activity to use with making inferences is to make copies of a passage from a biography or autobiography and have students make inferences about the author: gender, education, career, politics, life experiences, attitudes about life or other people. (The passage "Being Nice" in *The Big Picture* by Ben Carson elicits some fascinating responses.) If you use an excerpt from a work of fiction, first discuss the concept of **persona**—the idea that we all have an aspect of our personality that is discernible or public. It is possible to discern the persona of an author of fiction, though this is a more difficult task than determining the persona of a more visible celebrity, such as an actor or wrestler. An evocative passage from a Stephen King novel can reveal the author's persona. On a deeper level, however, does the passage really reveal the author's inner, private self? That brings us to critical reading and unraveling the public and private layers, the truth and the propaganda.

"To read well, that is to read true books in a true spirit, is a noble exercise, and one that will task the reader more than any exercise which the customs of the day esteem. It requires a training such as the athletes underwent, the steady intention almost of the whole life to this object."—Henry David Thoreau

Introduction

- Begin by reading aloud *The Wretched Stone* by Chris van Allsburg. It is a fictional account of the log of the captain of the *Rita Anne*. The sailing vessel encountered a treacherous storm and nearly sank because the crew was mesmerized by a mysterious stone; consequently, they refused to do their work. Do not give a synopsis. Simply explain that this book, written and illustrated by the same Caldecott Medal winner who wrote *Jumanji,* is written on two levels. One level is for children who love a good adventure story. The other level is for critical readers who understand figurative language and the consequences of poor decisions.
- On the board write, "The wretched stone is _____." Tell them that, as they listen to the story, they should try to discover what the wretched stone symbolizes. They should consider the writer's clues, their own experiences, and their logic.
- The wretched stone represents a TV (or a computer monitor). Although the detailed description is helpful, there is no dead give-away. Resist the temptation to reveal the answer. If the students do not get it, have them write down the details and share the puzzle with their friends. Some clever students may even go on the Internet to discover the answer, or you may have a good critical listener who can solve the mystery in class.
- Explain that many things are written on different levels and, to comprehend them, an active learner must use a higher level of thinking: critical thinking.

Input

- Next, show the overview of the chapter. Since there is so much important material, a view of the big picture will provide a focus.

Critical Reading

- ⊕ Does the material contain facts, opinions, or a combination of both?

- ⊕ What is the author's purpose?

- ⊕ What is the author's tone?

- ⊕ How strong are the data and evidence?

- ⊕ Is the author biased?

- ⊕ How is connotative language used?

- ⊕ How is figurative language used?

Is the Material Fact or Opinion?

- Give the students an editorial from the local paper. Have them list facts, opinions, or a combination, and decide how effective the essay is. Have them look for words and phrases mentioned in the text: *in my view*; *possibly*; *in my opinion*.

What Is the Author's Purpose?

- To help students focus on an author's purpose, give them the mnemonic device PIE: persuade, inform, and entertain. Then have the students consider a passage from the text. Point out that some of the best writing includes a combination. For example, some of the most effective persuasive writing is also very entertaining and may contain some important facts. A well-written movie review may be an example you would choose to discuss.

Tone

- There are many different ways to say, "I love you," and the inflection of the voice, **tone**, can be important in discerning the true meaning. After considering the examples in the text, have students study the table of "Words Frequently Used to Describe Tone" in their textbook. Be sure to discuss definitions of any unfamiliar words. (This is good opportunity to sneak in a vocabulary lesson with words such as *austere, bombastic, elegiac, facetious, flamboyant, iconoclastic, irreverent, nostalgic, pompous, whimsical.*) Also have the students consider the contrast in tone in Reading 32: *Bugs in Your Pillow* and Reading 33: *The Biodiversity Crisis*.

Is the Author Biased?

- Make a transparency of the following for students to see the details presented. Remind students to ask critical questions. Even when the data and evidence are available, they are frequently suppressed.

- In 1948, researchers at Saranac Laboratory for research in tuberculosis sent a memo to Owens-Illinois reporting that their findings for Kaylo, a brand name for asbestos, revealed less than favorable results. "I realize that our findings regarding Kaylo are less favorable than anticipated. However, since Kaylo is capable of producing asbestosis, it is better to discover it now in animals rather than later in industrial workers. Thus the company, being forewarned, will be in a better position to institute adequate control measures for safeguarding exposed employees and protecting its own interests." (Source: November 16, 1948, memorandum to Owens-Illinois from Arthur J. Vorwald, M.D., director of Saranac Laboratory for research in tuberculosis.)

- In 1956, however, an advertisement by Owens-Illinois Glass stated: "Easy fabrication—Kaylo-20 Block can be cut, scored or sawed with ordinary tools of the trade. Light weight, pleasant handling and non-irritating and non-toxic nature contribute to worker well-being on the job." (Source: Owens-Illinois Glass Company advertisement, 1956.)

How Strong Are the Data and Evidence?

- This chapter is an excellent one to use visuals to show how propaganda is used. For example, the "Man of the Year" photograph on the cover of *Time* magazine (January 4, 1993) depicts then President-elect Bill Clinton with the "M" in Time positioned behind his head so that it looks like horns—implying a devilish character. (Time editors were chided for this tactic.)
- Also, the February 21, 1994, issue—before any case went to trial—shows a demure Nancy Kerrigan in white, dancing freely, unsuspecting, while a sinister-looking Tonya Harding lurks in the shadowed background looking remarkably like a stalker.
- Because the press can manipulate public opinion, it is important for us to identify such tactics and critically think beyond the obvious.
- Remind students that seeing is not believing. When the film *Rainman* was released, receiving wide acclaim, *Newsweek* ran an article with a photograph of actors Tom Cruise and Dustin Hoffman dressed in formal attire and smiling. The caption said that the reason the movie was so successful was because of the chemistry between the two actors. The implication was that the actors were at the same formal function, sharing a joke, when in reality Tom Cruise was photographed in California, and Dustin Hoffman was photographed in New York, and the images were manipulated.

Connotative Language

- Remind students of the definitions of **imply** and **infer.** Explain the textbook definition of connotation and denotation. You may also want to explain that a euphemism is a word with a positive connotation. Write the following on the board: Freedom fighter/Terrorist
- Explain that one evokes a positive image, while the other creates revulsion. The connotation of a word, then, is an important factor in advertisement and political propaganda.
- If time allows, you may have the students consider the evolution of the terms for abortion. Originally, those against abortion were called *anti-abortionists*. Those for abortion were *pro-abortionists*. This confused some people because the prefix *anti-* is negative, but they felt their cause was positive. When they renamed themselves *pro-life*, the opponents then renamed themselves *pro-choice*. In both cases, *pro* is positive, as are the terms *life* and *choice*. In a sense, this was a way to even the "playing field" between both sides.

Figurative Language

- Use the following handout as a guided note-taking activity. Students should create or discover a second example from their personal reading.

Figurative Language

Term	Definition	Example	Example
Metaphor		*The bridge at nighttime was a diamond necklace on black velvet.*	
Simile		*The bridge at nighttime was like a diamond necklace on black velvet.*	
Personification		*This computer tries to sabotage me on a daily basis.*	
Hyperbole		*The first question is worth a million points.*	
Oxymoron		*"Thunderous silence or sweet sorrow."*	

Chapter 7: Organizing Ideas

"Read, read, read. Just like a carpenter who works as an apprentice and studies a master, read!"—William Faulkner

Introduction

- This chapter introduces five strategies for students to become effective, active learners. You may want to teach these techniques at the beginning of the semester in conjunction with Chapter 1: Active Reading and Thinking Strategies. As one student recently observed, "Why didn't they teach us this a long time ago?"
- Ask students what strategies they anticipate will be discussed in this chapter. Ask who has a highlighter and uses it correctly on a regular basis. Explain that organization is difficult for many people, but everyone can learn to organize.
- Point out the continuing analogy of a student building a framework for knowledge. This step is critical to the construction of a solid framework. These strategies will help turn information into a "learnable" package and will be the mortar that holds it all
- together.

Input

- You may want to introduce this chapter during the first week of class.
- To acquaint students with the strategies, give them the guided note-taking handout on the next page. Be sure to eliminate the underlined and italicized answers before making the student copies. Then have the students write in the appropriate answers as you introduce each skill.
- Tell students that some research indicates that a student's ability to summarize is the single best predictor of his or her success in subsequent college-level courses.
- Throughout the course, give students a variety of opportunities to use all of the strategies presented in Chapter 7. Each time students use the strategies as a classroom activity always give them an opportunity to observe their classmate's results. Students learn best from observing other students' strategies.
- As you study paragraphs or longer passages, ask students to organize the information into an outline first, then a map. Start from simple examples to ones that are more complicated. Ask students to put their examples on the board. Explain that some will prefer the outline form, while others will prefer the map. This will depend on how they prefer to receive knowledge—their own particular learning style.

Organizing Ideas

Strategy	Explanation
Highlighting	Improves comprehension and recall and forces the reader to focus. <u>Be sure to read first, then highlight, and never highlight more that 20-30%.</u>
Annotating	Requires active reading and written responses as the reader reflects on content.
Paraphrasing	<u>Restating the ideas of the passage in your own words facilitates learning complicated material.</u>
Outlining	Assists in organizing information and pulling ideas together, particularly from two or more sources.
Mapping	
Conceptual Maps	Present ideas spatially and help visual learners.
Process Diagrams	Present steps, variables, or parts of a process.
Part and Function Diagrams	Present labeled drawings for the description and classification of physical objects.
Time Lines	Present sequence or order of events.
Summarizing	Presents a brief statement of key points, forcing the reader to condense ideas in his or her own words, thus facilitating recall.

Chapter 8: Improving and Adjusting Your Reading Rate

"If you read ten pages a day, you can read ten 300-page books a year."

—Judy Remsberg

Introduction

- Students frequently enjoy learning about reading rate. It is an activity which many college students feel will help them become the competition. Time management is often a critical element with college students, and improving their reading rate is appealing. Stress that, although a faster reading rate is not synonymous with greater comprehension, if they force themselves beyond their comfort zone, they may find that their comprehension can improve. Remind them that the best way to improve their reading rate is to, well, read. Reading for fifteen minutes a day will promote an increase in their speed and their comprehension.

Input

- To encourage those who are interested, offer some book "commercials" of very short books and novels with a lot of dialog that students can tackle in fifteen-minute chunks. After offering a brief synopsis, read a short passage to pique their interest. Some popular quick reads are listed below:

- *Early Autumn* by Robert B. Parker
- *The Notebook; A Walk in the Woods; The Rescue* by Nicholas Sparks
- *Tuesdays with Morrie* by Mitch Albom
- *Ellen Foster* by Kaye Gibbons
- *Ten Things I Wish I'd Known Before I Went Out into the Real World* by Maria Shriver
- *Gifted Hands; Think Big; The Big Picture* by Benjamin Carson, MD
- *Where the Heart Is* by Billie Letts
- *What Looks Like Crazy on an Ordinary Day* by Pearl Cleage
- *Walking Across Egypt* by Clyde Edgerton
- *The Hot Zone* by Richard Preston
- *The Brethren* by John Grisham
- *All That Remains* by Patricia Cornwell
- *Holes* by Louis Sachar
- *The Color of Water* by James McBride
- *A Child Called "It"* and *A Man Named Dave* by David Pelzer
- *Timeline* by Michael Crichton
- *Absolute Power* by David Baldacci
- *The Sisterhood of the Traveling Pants* by Ann Brashares
- *The Kite Runner* by Khaled Hosseini

Average Reading Rates

Reading Rate	Material	Level of Comprehension
Below 200 wpm	Poetry, legal documents, argumentative essays	100%
200-300 wpm	Textbooks, manuals, research documents	80-100%
300-500 wpm	Novels, paperbacks, newspapers, magazines	60-80%

Chapter 9: Reading and Evaluating Electronic Sources

"Everybody will have realized from personal experience how closely we are integrated psychologically with the instruments that serve us."—Sir Peter Medawar

Introduction

- Show the "wordles" on the next page to the students and ask them to determine the various meanings. (The wordles are word puzzles that require some critical thinking.
- Explain that when we read a book, we read linearly. However, when we read electronic sources, we are required to read and think differently, just as the students were required to do to solve the wordles.

Input

- Provide the process diagram on page 71 of the manual for students as a transparency for an overview of the chapter material.
- Use the guided note-taking activity on page 72 of the manual to discuss the various types of Web sites.
- On page 73 is a conceptual map to accompany the class discussion on evaluating a Web site.
- Finally, have students visit the following site at Virginia Tech to discern the accuracy of the Web sites presented:

  http://www.lib.vt.edu/help/instruct/evaluate/evaluating.html

Wordles

Gseg

Issue, issue, issue, issue, issue, issue, issue, issue, issue

Jack

T   I   M   E
      abde

Answers: Scrambled eggs; tennis shoes; jack-in-the-box; long time no see

Steps in Reading Electronic Sources

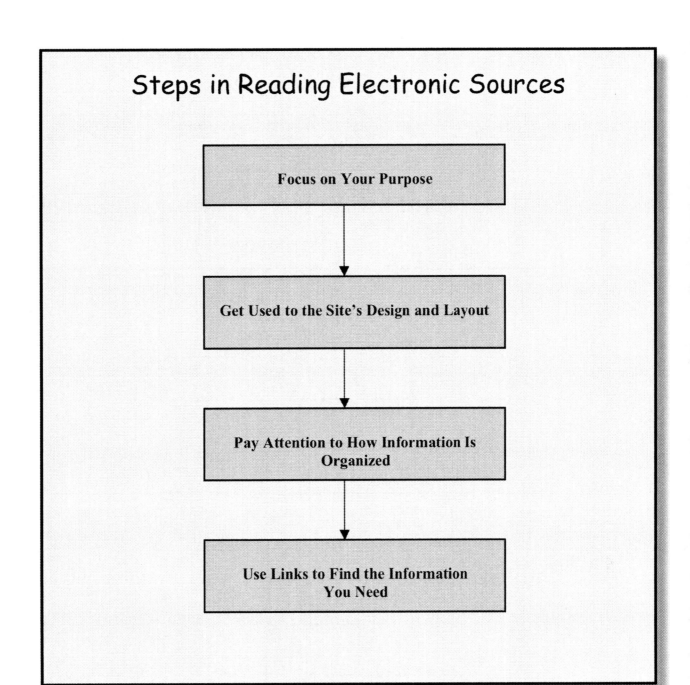

Types of Web Sites

Type	Purpose	Description	URL
_____	To present facts, information, and research data	May contain reports, statistical data, results of research studies, and reference material.	_____
News	_____ _____ _____ _____	Often supplements print newspapers, periodicals and television news programs.	_____
Advocacy	To promote a particular cause or point of view	_____ _____	.org
Personal	To provide information about an individual and his/her interests and accomplishments	_____ _____ _____ _____	_____
_____	To promote goods or services	May provide news and information related to their products.	_____

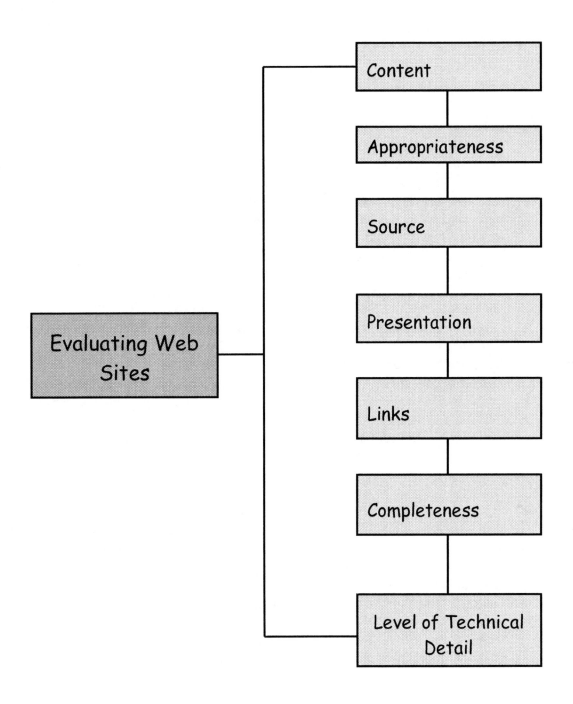

Chapter 10: Reading Across the Disciplines

"True wisdom comes to each of us when we realize how little we understand about life, ourselves, and the world around us."—Socrates

Introduction

- Relate the story of *The Ditch Digger's Daughters* by Yvonne Thornton with Jo Coudert. (A summary can be found at www.amazon.com) The father zealously searched for every opportunity to help his daughters get the education he never had. One bit of wisdom that he imparted to them to help them succeed in class was this—Find a rabbit! The daughters found his suggestion to be some of the best advice they had ever received. Explain to your students that "a rabbit" is someone sitting close to you who is making better grades. Observe what they are doing and mimic their efforts and study habits. When you catch up to them, look for a faster rabbit. There are always better ways to study.
- Explain that the different disciplines in college are very specialized and unique. Students will need to assemble a "tool bag" of skills and strategies to prepare successfully for each of their classes. Ask your students about the "tools" that athletes need for their various sports. What kind of tools do carpenters need? Car mechanics? How does this relate to tools needed for college coursework?
- Ask students to name their majors and survey the class to see if they know the names of the different disciplines available for study on campus.

Input

- Make an overhead of the following transparency. Write the names of the academic disciplines on the board. Ask students to decide in which category they believe the classes belong. This is a good opportunity for students to learn about the various courses on campus. Next, ask students to analyze the assignments and match them up with the correct disciplines.
- Take the time to do some general advising about class registration for the upcoming semester. Discuss various majors, pre-requisites, job opportunities, and required credentials. Bring in the college catalog and explain its format and the kinds of information found inside. Make an overhead of one course of study to show as an example.
- If students are undecided about their major, direct them to the available campus resource centers: career center, counseling center, transfer center.
- Students may find the following Web sites helpful in searching for career information: www.monster.com   www.careerbuilder.com
www. collegeboard.com/apps/careers/index   www.careerjournal.com

Sample Courses

Adolescent Behavior	Aging and Health
Microbiology	Engineering
Drafting	Drafting and Design
Photography	Geography
Western Civilization	Basic Horticulture Laboratory
African-American History	Nature Photography
Chemistry	Oceanography
Biology	Plant Anatomy
Calculus	Embryology of Vertebrates
Health and Nutrition	Human Anatomy and Physiology
Accounting	Herpetology
Business Law	Computer Engineering Design
Statistics	Computer Architecture
Computer Science	Beginning Painting
Print-Making	Women, Gender, and Culture
Renaissance Art	Sculpture
Anthropology	Criminology
Physics	Finance
Economics	Management
Marketing	Analytic Geometry
Linear Algebra	Juvenile Delinquency

Sample Assignments

1. Create a list of the major categories of behavior that affect international business.
2. Describe the culture differences between Arab nations and the U.S.
3. Calculate the total number of tickets people buy if they purchase three tickets every week of the year. If the tickets cost $1.00 and their total income is $25,000, what percent of income are they spending on lottery tickets?
4. Create a film involving two people and a surprise.
5. Explain the stages of photosynthesis in a plant.
6. Prepare a spreadsheet showing your purchases for the past week.
7. Describe the attitudes of the two groups of students involved in the study of depression.
8. Describe the important differences in the growth and development of plants and animals.
9. Design a container that holds a raw egg that can be dropped from a four-story height without damaging the egg.
10. Explain the five major types of damage that can affect hardware and software.

Part II: Readings in Academic Disciplines

Reading Level: 7

Introduction

- Write the word *urban* on the board and ask for a volunteer to define it. Next, write the word *legend* on the board and ask for a definition.
- Then ask students to consider what the medieval play *Everyman*, all of the Star Trek films, and the current movies *Urban Legends*, *Urban Legends II*, and *Urban Legends: The Final Cut* have to do with social sciences.
- Tell a local urban legend or show a brief clip from one of the recent films with the same name or ask if students know an urban legend—either one they think happened locally in the past few years or one they have heard passed down.
- Explain that these are considered "morality plays." http://riri.essortment.com/englishdrama_rjdz.htm will provide some background on medieval morality plays. Have the students read "The Hook" and "Kentucky Fried Rat." Have the students read them. You may have one or two students who will volunteer to read them aloud or you can have the students follow along as you read them.
- Instruct the students to then follow the steps to previewing the entire essay following the procedure in Part One. Next, have the student read the article.

Follow-Up

- Point out the tips mentioned that aid in the study of social sciences. Emphasize the need to consider what strategies work best for the students in a particular subject: Pay attention to terminology; understand explanations and theories; look for supporting evidence; make comparisons and connections; and make practical applications. Remind students not to highlight until after they have read the passage through once. Also, indicate that students can apply some of the strategies mentioned in chapter 7, which discusses tips for organizing ideas.
- Since a social-science course would encourage the students to compare and contrast, you may want to draw a Venn diagram (overlapping circles) on the board, and have them recall details without using their books. In the center, where the circles overlap, you would list the three common characteristics of urban legends: They serve as a warning, reflect social change, and instill fear and guilt. You may also want to mention that urban legends seem credible and have ironic twists. In addition, you will most likely need to explain irony, how it requires readers to make inferences, and that O.Henry's short stories provide some excellent opportunities to study stories with ironic twists.
- Next, have the students tell you some story details that could be placed in the remaining areas, either under the label "The Hook" or "Kentucky Fried Rat."

- With the Venn diagram on the board, ask students some of the following questions:

  - Does our local legend share any of the same characteristics?
  - Do any other legends you have heard or seen bear the same attributes?
  - When you heard some of these stories, did you believe they were true? If so, what made them credible, or believable, when you heard them?
  - Consider the possible origin of the stories, and speculate who might have first told such a story about "The Hook" or "Kentucky Fried Rat" or "Welcome to the World of AIDS."
  - Because research reveals that a student's ability to write succinct, accurate summaries is one of the best predictors of his or her success in subsequent college courses, tell the students to pretend that they have just read this chapter as part of a sociology assignment and that they now need to prepare a summary.

Summary

Who: Sociologists
What: Theorize that urban legends are morality plays
When: Currently
Where: In our culture
Why: To serve as a warning; to reflect social change; to instill fear and guilt
How: By providing stories with an ironic twist with credible details that seem to have been passed on recently by friends.

Then have the students compose a summary in 50 words or less.

Sample:

Some sociologists theorize that urban legends are actually "morality plays" currently being spread in our culture to serve as a warning, to reflect social change, and to instill fear and guilt by providing stories that seem believable, albeit ironic, and are passed down by friends. (45 words)

Then have students pare down the summary to 30 words or less.

Sociologists believe current urban legends are morality plays, shared by friends, that warn, reflect social change, and instill fear and guilt by using believable details and ironic endings. (29 words)

Quiz: Urban Legends

True/False

___1. Urban legends are false stories that appear true.

___2. Urban legends are stories with ironic twists.

___3. Urban legends lack credibility because of their lack of believable details.

Multiple Choice

___4. The urban legends in the essay share what major points with all other urban legends?

    a. Provide warnings about eating fast food; demonstrate the inability of most people to make good decisions; instill a sense of humor about the absurd.
    b. Serve as entertainment for a serious subject; relate a change in our eating habits; instill fear and guilt in women.
    c. Serve as warnings; related to social change; instill fear and guilt in the reader or listener.
    d. Serve as a form of entertainment; serve as a lesson about how cruel humans can be to each other; serve as an example of the irresponsibility of the younger generation.

___5. According to folklorist, Jan Brunvand, urban legends are most often passed down

    a. from parents to children because parents want them to make responsible decisions.
    b. from friend to friend.
    c. from business competitors.
    d. from religious leaders in the community.

Reading Level: 10

Introduction

- Write the word *flirting* on the board. Ask how many of the students flirt? How many have been the recipient of someone's flirtatious game? After they have explored the previewing steps, have your students share some ideas about the questions listed:

    - Why do people flirt?
    - Who takes the lead in flirting?
    - What are sexual semaphores?
    - What are some of the findings in the *Psychology Today* article that you find surprising?

Follow-Up

- Use the guided note-taking activity on the next page to accompany the discussion of the passage.
- Following the reading of the article, explain that they need to consider strategies they would use to study this passage for a psychology class. Divide the class into four groups and give them the following assignment:
    - Provide a conceptual map to use as a study guide.
    - Create a summary in 30 words or less.
    - Develop a mnemonic device and visual to recall details from the essay.
    - Make review cards with key concepts.
    - Anticipate an essay question. Using bulleted items, list the points which the group members would include in their answer.

Sexual Semaphores

Men	Women
Usually men are the ones summoned.	*Women initiate flirting two out of three times.*
Stick out chest and struts and appears dominant	*Primp, preen, giggle, pout, nod, lick lips*
Lower head	Lower head
Direct eye contact	*Direct eye contact for long periods*
Sustained smiling	Sustained smiling
Never wholly dominate	*Control pace by escalating and de-escalating flirtation's progression*
Tend to follow the woman's lead	*Learn flirtatious leadership roles early*

Quiz: The New Flirting Game

True/False

____1. According to the article, flirtations are most often initiated by men.

____2. Neither women nor men wholly dominate in flirtatious encounters.

____3. Some cultures use a coy smile as a flirtatious gesture more frequently than others.

Multiple Choice

____4. The women who attract the most men are those

      a. with the most symmetrical features.
      b. with the best hip-to-waist ratio.
      c. who send out the most signals.
      d. who send out no signals.

____5. Which statement about flirting is not true?

      a. There are some behaviors that are universal among women.
      b. Covering her mouth is not necessarily submissive for a woman.
      c. A woman may give signals that are both submissive and dominant.
      d. During a flirtatious encounter, men usually feel powerful.

Reading Level: 7

Introduction

- Remind the students of the tips for reading ethnic studies: Pay attention to the cultural context; be open to new viewpoints; make generalizations cautiously.
- Introduce Ben Carson's story by reading aloud the acrostic from his book, *Think Big* (Carson, B. *Think Big*, Zondervan Publishing House) which reveals his philosophy.
- Ask if anyone has heard Dr. Carson speak or has read any of his books (*Gifted Hands*, *Think Big*, or *The Big Picture*) or seen him on TV specials. If so, some students may be able to share some information before the class previews.

Follow-Up

- While in medical school, Carson learned to give the college instructors more than they asked for, so he frequently did in-depth research on a particular subject. Ask students to search the Web for additional information on Carson's life and work and then report to the class.

Summary

Who: Ben Carson, head of pediatric neurosurgery at Johns Hopkins Hospital
What: Shares anecdotes of his experiences and encourages people to be positive and pro-active.
When: Throughout his career
Where: In speeches and writings
Why: Because he overcame some major obstacles in his own life
How: Through the support and discipline imposed by his mother, he now accepts a self-imposed obligation to act as a role model to black youngsters.

Sample:

Because he was able to overcome financial and academic obstacles in his own life through the support and discipline imposed by his mother, Ben Carson, present head of pediatric neurosurgery at Johns Hopkins Hospital, frequently shares anecdotes of his life and career to encourage all young people to become positive and pro-active. Carson feels a special obligation to act as a role model to black youngsters.

Quiz: Coming Into My Own

True/False

____1. Benjamin Carson's mother was a major positive influence in his life.

____2. Because of his position as a doctor, Carson has not been the recipient of racial prejudice.

____3. Because of the state of race relations today, Carson sees no hope for the future.

Multiple Choice

____4. Carson feels that many of the pressing racial problems will be solved when

      a.   more people are college-educated.
      b.   computer technology gives people a more global view.
      c.   medicine improves mental health professions.
      d.   minorities refuse to look to others to improve their situations.

____5. According to Carson, "The only pressure I felt during my internship, and in the years since, has been a

      a.   self-imposed obligation to act as a role model for Black youngsters.
      b.   need to educate white medical professionals.
      c.   need to pay back exorbitant loans incurred during medical school.
      d.   constant need to prove himself as a qualified professional.

Reading Level: 12

Introduction

- Begin by asking students in the class to name the different reality shows they have watched. What characteristics do these shows have in common? Do reality shows treat men and women differently? Do students feel that people are influenced by the behaviors they see on these shows? Do the shows reflect reality as the students have experienced it, or do students believe these shows portray only Hollywood fantasies?

- Ask students to read the article then consider the following questions:

  o Do reality shows present a danger to viewing audiences? Why or why not?
  o Do the shows seem contrived or are they true to life?
  o Should reality shows have more stringent standards?

Follow-Up

- Remind students that some articles addressing communication/media concerns frequently analyze an issue, point out the problems, then suggest possible solutions. Ask the class to brainstorm details from the article without using the text as a guide. Write the details they recall on the board. Ask the class to analyze the items on the board and point out those that specify problems. Circle these. Then ask students to point out the details that suggest a solution. Draw a box around these. Finally, to create organization, have student fill in the table on the next page.

- Ask the class to identify the parts of the argument that are presented in this selection. What is the claim? What kinds of support does the author give as evidence? Consider the statistics and quotes that the author includes. Are these effective? Is the argument convincing? Does the article mention opposing views? Remind students that argumentation teaches them to question, analyze, respond, evaluate, and synthesize. All of these ways of responding to information involve critical thinking and problem solving. When students argue a position, they learn to examine the positions of others—the quality of their opinions, the quality of their logic, the fairness of their assumptions. They also learn how to close the gap between themselves and those who are different—those who disagree. They learn to recognize and respect disagreement and learn the value of establishing common ground.

- Ask students to consider censorship of television and movies. Do they believe censorship to be beneficial? Why or why not? Are they worried about the influence of reality television programs on children? What could parents do?

Problems of Reality Shows

Solutions

Quiz: Reality TV: Race to the Bottom

True/False

____1. According to the article, most reality shows honor good behavior and honesty among the contestants.

____2. The author isn't too concerned about lingering effects of reality shows because she understands the temporary nature of most television programs and understands that these shows will soon be replaced by another trend.

____3. Studies show that profanity and sexual references are occurring more frequently in recent reality series.

Multiple Choice

____4. Which is *not* a characteristic of reality shows?

       a. Reality shows thrive on one-upmanship.
       b. Reality shows reward contestants for conniving behavior.
       c. Reality shows have more explicit content than many other programs.
       d. Contestants are fully informed of all possible consequences.

____5. Which of the following is a factual statement about reality shows?

       a. Reality shows are a form of mental cruelty.
       b. Reality television is very harmful for the contestants.
       c. Reality shows constitute 13% of broadcast programming.
       d. Children are strongly influenced by the contestants on reality shows.

Reading Level: 11

Introduction

- Write the following words on the board: *snail-mail, technophobe, teleshopping, chocoholic, cloning, hoody.* Ask the students to define these terms and to name more examples of newly coined words.
- Discuss the definition of the word *etymology.* Explain how to recognize and read an etymology in the dictionary. *Assassin* or *sabotage* are good choices. (*Assassin* once meant a user of hashish in Arabic. A hashish user would more likely kill for money and disappear back to an opium den. A *sabot* was a French work boot that was used to jam machinery, giving workers a much-needed break during the long working hours of the early Industrial Revolution.)
- One of the most comprehensive English dictionaries is the *Oxford English Dictionary,* published by the Oxford University Press in England. Students can visit their online site (www.askOxford.com) to find quotes, questions, and answers about words.
- Explain that many new words are specific to a sport, a job, or to a particular area of science or technology. Point out the title of this selection and ask students to guess the topic before reading the introduction.

Follow-Up

- Divide the students into groups. Give each group an index card and assign them one of the words mentioned in the article: *weapons-grade, kamikazes, grunts, Ground Zero, snafu, basket case.* Ask the students to locate the word in the article, read the sentence carefully, and define the term. Challenge them to come up with their own example of a sentence using the new word. Ask one person from each group to read aloud their sentence.
- Conclude by asking the class to ponder the title of this selection. Ask if someone can explain why the title is a clever choice.

Quiz: War: The Mother of All Words

True/False

____1. From the article, you can infer that weapons-grade charisma refers to personality that has a powerfully magnetic appeal.

____2. The phrase "the mother of all battles" is attributed to Saddam Hussein.

____3. The meaning of "Ground Zero" has changed since the advent of the war on terrorism.

Multiple Choice

____4. All of the following words were mentioned *except*
   a. Wahhabism.
   b. chad.
   c. agroterrorism.
   d. shuicide bomber.

____5. Which statement does the information in this selection support?

   a. Once a word is included in a dictionary, its definition always remains the same.
   b. The American Dialect Society holds a serious contest every year to determine which words to add to dictionaries.
   c. The task of deciding which words to include in dictionaries is a relatively simple one.
   d. Although some new words have arisen from the war against terrorism, there are relatively few in comparison to other wars.

Reading Level: 11

Introduction

- What do Romeo and Juliet, Anthony and Cleopatra, Pyramis and Thisbe have in common?
- How about Tom Cruise and Nicole Kidman, Jennifer Aniston and Brad Pitt, Meg Ryan and Russell Crowe?
- Students will mention that these are paired lovers, some still together, some not, some who met with tragic endings.
- Ask if any other famous love stories come to mind.
- Then have them brainstorm with you to complete a Venn diagram comparing and contrasting love and infatuation.

Follow-Up

- Ask students to read the passage silently and be prepared to recall details. Give them a time limit to complete the reading.
- Following the reading, have the students close their textbook and ask students in round-robin fashion to recall details. As they suggest a type of love, create a category on the board and list the characteristics of each as they are given. Do not editorialize at this point.
- When everyone has had a chance to answer, ask the students to open their books and verify their observations.
- Ask if anyone has a mnemonic device to remember the six types of loves. If no one does, suggest ELAMPS.
- Finally, ask the students to participate in the guided note-taking activity to organize their notes and to learn the psychology terms and definitions.

Type of Love	Clarification
_____	1. Sensitive to physical imperfections. 2. Often feels unfulfilled. 3. Focuses on beauty and physical attraction. 4.
Ludus	1. 2. 3. 4.
Storge	1. 2. 3. 4.
Pragma	1. Practical and traditional. 2. Seeks a relationship that will work. 3. Views love as a useful relationship, one that. makes the rest of life easier. 4. These relationships rarely _____.
_____	1. Characterized by elation and depression. 2. Loves intensely and worries intensely about the loss of love. 3. Obsessive and possessive. 4. Poor self-image.
_____	1. 2. 3. 4.

Quiz: Lovers

True/False

____1. Eros lovers tend to be shallow people focused mainly on physical attributes.

____2. Ludic lovers need to feel controlled by their partners.

____3. Pragma lovers are characterized by intense highs and lows.

Multiple Choice.

____4. The type of love exemplified by Ghandi, Jesus, and Buddha is

        a. agape.
        b. pragma.
        c. storge.
        d. ludic.

____5. The author most likely would agree with all of the following *except*

        a. Each of the six loves can combine with others to form new and different patterns.
        b. Different styles attest to the fact that different people want different things.
        c. Each person seeks satisfaction in a unique way.
        d. Storge love is lifeless and boring.

Reading Level: 11

Introduction

- Mention some of the sayings and customs associated with American weddings: *Something old/ Something new/ Something borrowed/ Something blue*. Shivaree; Tin cans tied to cars; Throwing rice; Announcing the banns;
- Ask students about their own weddings or personal experiences with weddings. Are there students from culturally diverse backgrounds who are willing to share their wedding memories? How have wedding ceremonies changed over the years?
- Share the story of *Fiddler on the Roof* with your class. Talk about the struggle that Tevia (the father) had when each of his daughters broke with tradition over their marriages.

Follow-Up

- Ask students to work together in pairs to answer the matching exercise on pages 239 - 240 in their text.
- Then have students recreate this information in an outline form (see next page) as a memory aid for study.
- Suggest that students prepare review cards listing the name of the religion on one side and the corresponding wedding traditions on the other.
- Finally, ask students to determine what all of these different traditions have in common.

Wedding Traditions

I. **African Methodist Episcopalian**
   A. _____
   B. _____

II. **Catholicism**
   A. _____
   B. _____
   C. _____

III. **Hellenic Orthodoxy**
   A. _____
   B. _____
   C. _____

IV. **Islam**
   A. _____
   B. _____

V. **Judaism**
   A. _____
   B. _____

VI. **Sikhism**
   A. _____
   B. _____
   C. _____

Quiz: To Love and To Cherish

True/False

___1. Couples sometimes mix traditions from several different cultures for their own wedding.

___2. A unity candle is sometimes used in a Catholic wedding to symbolize the union of two individuals from different religions and cultures.

___3. The bride and groom in a Jewish wedding actually sign a contract about their behavior.

Multiple Choice

___4. Wedding traditions of all the following religions are mentioned *except*

     a. Islam.
     b. Buddhism.
     c. Christian.
     d. Sikhism.

___5. One African wedding tradition involves

     a. breaking a wine glass.
     b. pouring water on the ground.
     c. wearing crowns of beaded circles.
     d. walking around an altar table 3 times and sipping from a glass of wine.

Reading Level: 7

Introduction

- Ask students to discuss American views toward tattooing. How do their grandparents feel? Their parents? Employers? When or where is tattooing not acceptable? Why have tattoos become more prominent in recent years? What reasons do students give for getting tattoos?

- Along this same line, talk to students about rites of passage. How does American culture acknowledge the transition to different stages of life? Students may mention such events as graduations, sweet-sixteen parties, religious celebrations, driving privileges, drinking and smoking age requirements, and achievements in scouting, sports, or other organizations. Next, ask students to discuss the age requirements for tattoos in this country.

- Remind students about some of the tips for studying anthropology: Pay attention to terminology, focus on patterns of behavior, make comparisons between and among groups and cultures, and relate the reading to real-life situations.

- This is an excellent opportunity to introduce the classic, *Moby Dick* by Herman Melville. Read the excerpt from chapter 3 that describes Queequeg, a South Sea Islander who is covered with tattoos. (Queequeg befriends the main character Ishmael.)

Follow-Up

- After students have read the selection, ask them to recall as many details as possible without looking at their texts. Circle the room in round-robin fashion until they have exhausted all of their answers. Ask them to open their texts to see if they have included the most important events.

Summary

Who: Young men and women
What: Undergoing tattooing
When: At the onset of adulthood
Where: Samoa
Why: Symbol of rite of passage as well as status
How: Highly respected tattooist
Sample:

Samoan men and women undergo tattooing by highly respected tattooists as a traditional part of their cultures that marks their passage to adulthood.

Quiz: Peti's Malu: Traditions of Samoan Tattooing

True/False

____1. Tattooing is an easily learned art in Samoa.

____2. Samoan custom requires that men must endure pain as part of the rite of passage to adulthood.

____3. Female daughters of royalty are tattooed with a malu, a special symbol that looks like a rhombus.

Multiple Choice

____4. Tattooists are often highly respected and much feared in Samoa because

        a. they are highly educated.
        b. they are very wealthy.
        c. they have control over the kind of design which each Samoan is allowed to wear.
        d. Samoans believe they hold power over life and death when they are performing their art.

____5. Tattooing of males requires a longer time than females because

        a. males have more tattoos than females do.
        b. females can withstand pain better than males can.
        c. the tattoos of males consist of very thin lines.
        d. females need less time for their skin to heal.

Reading Level: 13

Introduction

- Write the word *basketball* on the board. Ask students to decide if playing basketball is the same when a player is idly shooting "hoops," when playing a neighborhood "pick-up" game, when playing for a school team, or when playing professionally. Are these situations different? If so, what distinguishes one from the others?

- Talk about some professional basketball, baseball, or football players. What do the students know about them? What qualifications do the players have? What are the chances for high school athletes to go on and become professional players?

- Ask students to think about crowd behavior at games. How do games feature in our society? This is a good opportunity to talk about the Olympic games and trace the history of the Olympics. Students may be familiar with some of the political factors affecting past Olympic games and the athletes.

- Mention some of the notable movies that have focused on sports or sports teams. Students may be familiar with such movies as *Friday Night Lights*, *Rudy*, *The Natural*, *Greatest Game Ever Played*, *Hoosiers*, and *Radio*. Ask students to consider the similarities among the movies. Conclude with a copy from the library of the best-seller, *Bleachers,* by John Grishom. Read the back cover aloud. Invite students to read this book for extra credit.

Follow-Up

- Direct the students to read the selection a second time and circle the transitions that are used in the selection. Ask students to decide upon the main pattern of organization used for this selection. Ask them to explain their choice.

- Divide students into four groups. Assign each group a section of the article. Ask the groups to analyze each section and make a map that portrays the similarities and/or differences mentioned in the section. Then give the groups time to display their maps and report their findings.

- Make a transparency of the following page. Remind students of the differences among play, leisure, art, and work. Ask students to list the various activities mentioned in the article and decide how each should be classified. Ask students to fill in as many characteristics as possible from memory. Then give them time to scan the article to fill in the blanks.

Play, Leisure, and Culture

Country	Activity	Classification	Characteristics
America			
Japan			
India			
Europe			
Ukraine			

Quiz: Play, Leisure, and Culture

True/False

____1. According to this selection, play and leisure are not always the same.

____2. It is possible for anthropologists to learn much about a culture by studying its games and sports .

____3. Americans and Japanese both play the game of baseball with great passion, utilizing the same strategies and the same sense of competition.

Multiple Choice

____4. Men's wrestling in India involves

      a. the value of "doing your own thing."
      b. the ability to achieve and maintain team harmony.
      c. a strong link with spiritual development and a measure of strict self-discipline.
      d. competition that seeks to bring about the flow of blood or even death.

____5. Play and leisure can be distinguished from other activities by the fact that they

      a. seek to create a work of art.
      b. have no direct, useful, or practical purpose for the participant.
      c. can also be considered as work.
      d. are necessary activities that involve ordinary life.

Reading Level: 13.5

Introduction

- Remind students of the strategies they should use when reading about issues in education: Pay attention to issues; realize that measurement and assessment are important; look for trends and innovations; and pay attention to the multicultural aspects of education.

- Ask for some brainstorming concerning current issues in education.

- If this is a year for a local election of representatives in the state capital, ask what candidates are running and what is their stand on particular issues in education. You may want to suggest that the students read about the issues and attend a debate to see if the candidates' agenda really includes concerns about education.

- Selections 10 and 11 are paired readings that offer an opportunity for a class debate. Ask students to preview and then read both selections. Have them note emotional words that are used and ask them to look for examples of obvious bias. While using or adapting the debate format, allow the volunteers to prepare their arguments, and have the rest of the students serve as the panel of judges. As they read and then hear the two sides of the debate, they can fill in the comparison/contrast map in the textbook.

Debate Format

Affirmative: States the need for a change. (Schools should be year round.)

Negative: States the need for maintaining the status quo. (School should not be year round.)

- Eight minutes: First Affirmative constructive. (Establishs a need for change, tells why, and explains how.)

- Three minutes: Cross-examination by the second negative speaker. (Asks questions and looks for flaws in the first constructive.)

- Eight minutes: First negative constructive. (Explains why the affirmative argument is flawed and why the status quo is fine.)

- Three minutes: Cross-examination by the first affirmative speaker. (This gives the second affirmative constructive time to prepare.)

- Eight minutes: second affirmative constructive. (Beats down the first negative constructive's argument and elucidates on what partner has expressed.)

- Three minutes: Cross-examination by first[t] negative constructive.

- Eight minutes: Second negative constructive. (Explains why his or her side is right.)

- Three minutes: Cross-examination by second affirmative constructive.

- Rebuttal: Five minutes for each: 1NC; 1AC; 2NC; 2AC (This is similar to the closing arguments in a court case.)

- Following the debate, the class will vote on the winner of the debate.

Summary

An alternative to the debate is summary writing. Following the Who, What, When, Where, Why, How format, have students summarize the selection in 50 words or less. For example:

Who: Educators
What: Should adopt a year-round school policy
When: Presently
Where: Nationwide
Why: Beneficial to students
How: Careful planning with committed parents and teachers

Sample:

Through careful planning and the commitment of parents and teachers, educators should adopt a year-round school policy nationwide because schools need reorganization and because the benefits extend to students as well as to the community.

Quiz: Should Students Attend School Year Round? Yes

True/False

____1. The ten-month school-year plan originated because an agricultural society needed children and young people to help with the farm.

____2. The "hospitality industry" to which the author referred comprises hotels, restaurants, theme parks, and museums.

____3. Because the author is a school principal, the reader does not need to read critically to detect bias.

Multiple Choice

____4. According to the author, who will benefit from year-round schools?

   a. Day-care centers.
   b. Hospitality industry.
   c. Summer camps.
   d. Students.

____5. With which statement would the author most disagree?

   a. Most observers of American public education recognize the need for change.
   b. The one group that does not need to be convinced of the benefit of year-round school is the teachers.
   c. Lower-income parents understand that year-round school will benefit their children.
   d. Like any change, year-round school is likely to fail if not done right.

Reading Level: 10

Introduction

- Ask the students if they could change three things about public education, what would these be? Give students time to create their personal list, and then have them brainstorm and offer some ideas. Look for some organization and arrange the ideas in a conceptual map.

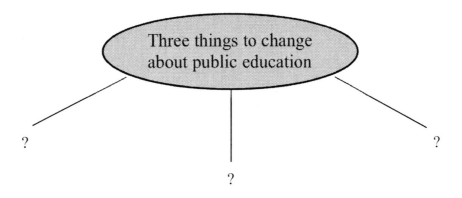

Follow-Up

- Ask students for examples of emotional words and obvious bias. Give them an opportunity to share their ideas on the advantages/disadvantages map on the following page.

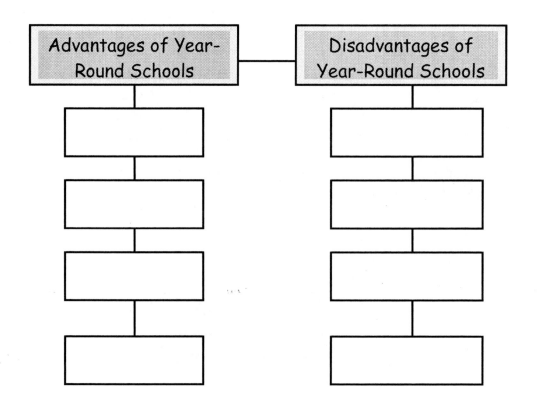

Quiz: Should Students Attend School Year Round? No

True/False

___1. The author agrees with researchers who claim that the breaks in year-round schools would prevent more forgetfulness and require less review.

___2. A major concern of the author is the effect of hot summers on children forced to attend school in classrooms without air conditioning.

___3. According to the author, good teaching helps to increase students' retention of material and decrease the amount of review time needed.

Multiple Choice

___4. According to the author, the key question concerning a change to year-round school:

        a. Will the calendar change improve student education?
        b. Can taxpayers afford the change?
        c. Will school boards still be able to recruit teachers?
        d. Can the public study the effects first before implementing the change?

___5. With which statement would the author most agree?

        a. More money, not time, makes better schools.
        b. An air-conditioned environment, not more time, makes better schools.
        c. Year-round school supporters are child advocates.
        d. More time in school does not necessarily make a more successful student.

Reading Level: 8

Introduction

- Tell students the story of Pat Conroy who, in his book, *The Water Is Wide*, relates the true account of a year of teaching on one of the coastal islands of South Carolina. The students he taught knew almost nothing but their narrow, impoverished lives. By getting to know them personally, he was able to bring about a radical change in their lives by championing education on this island.

- Ask students to imagine the difficulties facing children who enter school knowing little or no English and who must move from place to place and school to school lives because their parents must follow jobs.

- Bring to class a copy of *Raising Nuestros Ninos: Bring Up Latino Children in a Bicultural World* by Gloria Rodriguez. Rodriguez has written an extensive child-care manual in an effort to help Latino parents prepare their children for success in the world.

Follow-Up

- After reading the first few paragraphs, ask students to anticipate what will happen with Michael. Next, read the following statements and ask students to respond (anticipating the story's events). Following the reading, ask the students to respond again to the same statements. Did their responses change?

  1. This teacher is a caring teacher.
  2. This teacher is well-versed in educational theory.
  3. This teacher feels confident of her abilities.
  4. This teacher will be successful with her students.
  5. This teacher is an excellent teacher.

- After students have previewed and read the article, ask them to list and discuss the reasons why this teacher didn't know her student's real name.

- Talk about chronological order as an organizational pattern of development. Help students create a visual representation of the events of the story mentioned in the article. Use the diagram on the next page as a guide. Remind students that this is a good way to prepare for an essay test.

- What other relationships do students see in the article? Point out the paragraphs where the teacher contrasts herself with her student. What are some of the differences that she mentions?

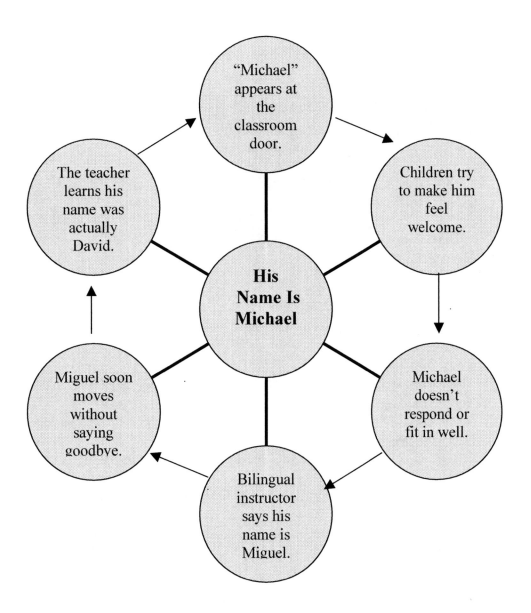

The teacher learns his name was actually David.

"Michael" appears at the classroom door.

Children try to make him feel welcome.

His Name Is Michael

Miguel soon moves without saying goodbye.

Bilingual instructor says his name is Miguel.

Michael doesn't respond or fit in well.

Quiz: His Name Is Michael

True/False

____ 1. Before Michael, this classroom teacher felt she was well prepared to handle any kind of challenge that students presented.

____ 2. Michael soon felt very comfortable, and he adapted well to the class in spite of the fact that he spoke no English.

____ 3. Michael didn't reveal his real name because he probably didn't connect school any known reality.

Multiple Choice

____ 4. According to the teacher,

    a. Michael was the name given to this student as his English name.
    b. Michael (David) probably expected and accepted that he was not important in the culture of the school.
    c. David had the power to correct his teacher; he just didn't wish to stand up for himself.
    d. she was not to blame for calling the student by the wrong name.

____ 5. This teacher learned the difficult lesson that being a good teacher

    a. is all about learning strategies to teach the curriculum and assess the students' progress.
    b. has much to do with building a sense of rapport and relationships with students.
    c. depends on the effectiveness of the administration.
    d. is almost impossible because of the large number of students in the classroom and the problems of teaching students who do not even speak English.

Reading Level: 12

Introduction

- On the board, write the following quotation by Dr. Caroline Gordon: "We do not judge great art. It judges us." Ask students what they think of when they hear the word "art." What do they think of as art? Next, ask them why they think people become artists, and what compels them to create.

- In *The Politics of Creativity*, Finley Eversole wrote, "In our society, at the age of five, 90 percent of the population measures 'high creativity.' By the age of seven, the figure has dropped to 10 percent. And the percentage of adults with high creativity is only two percent! Our creativity is destroyed not through use of outside force, but through criticism, innuendo." Explain that they are going to read about an artist who tapped into her creativity, who listened to a voice, and acknowledged the inspiration offered to her.

Follow-Up

- Point out to students the tips for reading arts/humanities/literature courses: Focus on values; pay attention to the medium; look for a message or an interpretation; read literature slowly and carefully.

- Explain to students that this reading exemplifies the type of reading found in an art history textbook. Art history courses typically have a high failure rate because students frequently fail to develop a study strategy. In order to be considered best in the competition, however, exemplary students create study cards with a picture and information about the artwork/artist.

- First, have students brainstorm as a class everything they can remember by going round robin along the rows and ask for input, no matter how insignificant the information may seem. Next, ask students to consider the information on the board and arrange it in some logical order. It may be chronological; it may be three categories such as *personal life, development of art, impact on the art world.* Give each student an index card and have them arrange the information on the card with some "illustration" to help anchor their minds to the artist and the work. Be sure to tell them to save space at the bottom for a summary.

- Have students summarize the article and share their samples.   To finish the card, they should write a summary at the bottom of the card.

Summary:

Who: Nampeyo
What: Preserved Hopi pottery designs and influenced Native American art
When: Late 19th and early 20th century
Where: Southwest Arizona
Why: Destiny; intrinsic talent; family influence
How: Studied with grandmother, then searched with anthropologists to find examples of the past to copy; eventually was inspired to create own designs

:Sample

During the late 19th and early 20th centuries in Southwest Arizona, Nampeyo, fascinated by the pottery of the past, studied with her grandmother and began to fine-tune her intrinsic talent to preserve the Hopi designs.   In addition, she searched with anthropologists to find past examples to copy.   Eventually, she was inspired to create her own designs and subsequently influenced Native American art.

Quiz: Shaping Her People's Heritage: Nampeyo (1852-1942)

True/False

___1. Nampeyo was first trained in pottery-making by her village shaman, or healer.

___2. A seed jar contained a seed from last year's corn crop to begin the new crop for the following year.

___3. While in Chicago, Nampyeo met great resistance to her art form because artists frequently fear competition from untrained Native Americans.

Multiple-Choice

___4. Traditional Native American ceramic arts had fallen into decline because

    a. "legitimate" artists did not recognize weak, untrained artists, and curators were discouraged from promoting Native American art forms.
    b. clay was scarce due to intense flooding, so raw materials were unavailable.
    c. mass production, coupled with the poverty of the area, promoted the purchase of inexpensive dishes and utensils from white traders.
    d. the Arizona state government forbade Native Americans from participating in free trade.

___5. Nampeyo's influence is recognized on all of the following *except*

    a. the creation of the Native American Arts and Crafts Board.
    b. literature of the Anasazi.
    c. pueblo artists.
    d. non-Native American interest in the purchase of the pottery.

Reading Level: 5

Introduction

- Tell students it took E.B. White two years to come up with the first line in *Charlotte's Web,* which is "Where's Papa going with that axe,' asked Fern." A first sentence can have a remarkable impact. Have students read the first sentence in the selection and determine the emotions the author evoked. What do you think his intent is?
- Remind students of the definition of *evocative* and ask them to watch for emotional language.
- Tell your students about the novel, *Bel Canto,* by Ann Patchett. This novel was the winner of the 2002 PEN/Faulkner Award and is a tender story of an opera singer and her audience, who were taken hostage in South America by a terrorist group. As the group and their captors live together for four months, the line between captive and captor often becomes confusing.

Follow-Up

- A good writer shows both sides of an issue. Ask students whether they feel the author shows two sides in this piece. Is this story biased? What evidence can they find to support two different arguments? Were the soldiers justified in "doing their duty"? When does duty end and responsibility begin, or are they the same?
- Have you ever been the recipient of someone's doing his or her duty? Is there a way to decide moral issues in time of war?

Time Line for Gregory

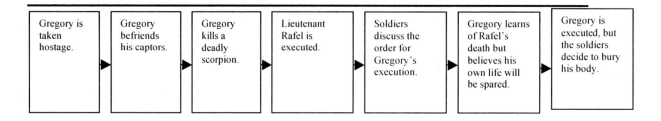

| Gregory is taken hostage. | Gregory befriends his captors. | Gregory kills a deadly scorpion. | Lieutenant Rafel is executed. | Soldiers discuss the order for Gregory's execution. | Gregory learns of Rafel's death but believes his own life will be spared. | Gregory is executed, but the soldiers decide to bury his body. |

Quiz: Gregory

True/False

___1. Gregory was taken hostage because he was a high-ranking military officer.

___2. The soldiers guarding Gregory were very lax about security because they knew Gregory was not a dangerous prisoner.

___3. Gregory felt a false sense of security about his safety because of the friendly relationship he had established with the guards.

Multiple Choice.

___4. Evidence of the camaraderie between Gregory and his guards can be seen in

    a. the teasing that went on between him and his captors.
    b. the guards' attitude that he was a "miserable, puny nobody."
    c. Gregory's disbelief that they wouldn't spare his life.
    d. the order for Gregory to wash their underwear while they discussed his execution.

___5. The author suggests that Gregory's death was

    a. an attempt to force the enemy to surrender.
    b. a message to the enemy of their superior strength in warfare.
    c. extremely important and highlighted in newspapers around the world.
    d. probably of little consequence to either side.

Reading Level: 4

Introduction

- Discuss the reading of poetry while paying attention to punctuation cues. Reading poetry is difficult for most students because they only do so once in a while and often don't think about what a poem is saying. Reading a poem well usually requires that students study it several times, reading it a different way each time. Suggest that your students read through the poem once, ignoring the line breaks and paying attention to the punctuation to get a sense of what is literally going on in the poem.

- The main focus of Linda Hogan's work concerns the traditional indigenous view of, and relationship to, the land, animals, and plants. While this is not the focus of this particular poem, discuss with your students the meaning of the word *indigenous* and ask them what it suggests about this poet.

Follow-Up

- After students have read the poem, point out that poetry often makes use of symbolism. Explain to students that they might have to stretch their imaginations, and really stretch, but poems usually invite symbolic meaning. There are also usually several levels of meaning to a poem. Two people might interpret a poem completely differently and both readings might have validity. That is NOT to say that students can inflict whatever meaning they like on a poem. There must be some textual evidence in the poem to support their view. Ask students if they see any symbols used in this poem.

- Another common poetic element is a central metaphor. Explain that some poems make a comparison between one thing and another, and understanding that comparison is the key to understanding the poem. Ask your students to go back to the poem to look for a central comparison.

- Finally, a theme is the basic message that the poem seems to be trying to convey, often a message about the world, or humanity, or nature, or sometimes something more specific. Ask students to choose one word that might relay the theme of this poem. Remind them that there is no one right answer.

- Ask students to use the first stanza as a model to compose their own short poem about themselves. Encourage students to be creative. This does not have to be about heritage but could reveal a secret side, a hidden desire, a perplexing issue.

> In my left pocket is a _____
> In my right pocket is a _____
> Don't worry. It's mine and not some _____'s.
> It belongs to a (man/woman) who _____

Quiz: The Truth Is

True/False

____1. The narrator of this poem is probably the mother of an aging Indian warrior.

____2. The narrator longs for peace of mind.

____3. The narrator is overwhelmed by the responsibilities that come with wealth.

Multiple Choice

____4. The phrase "who sleeps in a twin bed" might suggest that the narrator is

        a. probably a young person.
        b. sharing a bedroom.
        c. not in love at the present time.
        d. a very small person.

____5. The poem contains a metaphor in the line

        a. It's mine and not some thief's.
        b. I am a tree.
        c. My pockets are empty.
        d. We want amnesty.

Reading Level: 9

Introduction

- The article introduces a difficult dilemma. Explain the origin of the word *dilemma*: *di* = two and *lemma* = proposition. Sometimes a dilemma is a difficult choice between two equally attractive options; however, Selection 16 is about the decision to support the minimum wage or not.
- Poll the class about their view of the minimum wage law. How many work for minimum wage? What skills are required for these jobs? Are there any students who are paid less than the minimum wage? Why is this?

Follow-Up

- Using a transparency of the table on the next page , ask the students to brainstorm reasons to support or oppose the minimum wage law. Following the completion of the table, ask the students to vote for the most convincing arguments to determine if there is consensus. Ask them to decide where they stand on the issue using a scale of 1 – 20, using 1 if they feel very strongly against the minimum wage and 20 if they support it completely. Next, ask students to form a line, putting themselves in order from 1 - 20. Once they are in line, ask students at each end of the line to state their reasons for their choice. Continue down the line asking for opinions from each side. This is a strategy that helps students to listen to the opinions of others and develop understanding for the other point of view.
- Another option is to use Selection 16 as a subject for a debate on the topic of the minimum-wage law. Divide the class in half and ask each group to make a list of arguments both for and against a minimum wage. Ask for volunteers to lead the debate. (Use or modify the debate format previously discussed.)

Summary

Who: Employers and employees
What: The minimum-wage law was established to protect wages
When: From 1938 to present
Where:
Why: The minimum-wage law has many negative effects on employment
How: Controversy over benefits

Sample:

Although the minimum wage law was established in the in 1938 to protect employees' wages, it has resulted in many negative effects on employment and remains a controversial issue today.

Debate the Minimum Wage

Arguments for the Minimum Wage	Arguments Against the Minimum Wage

Evidence ?   Evidence?

Quiz: The Effects of the Minimum Wage

True/False

___1. The federal minimum wage was instituted in 1938 as a provision of the Fair Labor Standards Act.

___2. Once the minimum wage was set, it cannot be altered.

___3. Supporters of the minimum wage claim that it prevents exploitation of employees and helps people earn enough to support their families and themselves.

Multiple Choice

___4. Canadian research shows that, in the long run,

    a. increases in the minimum wage cause no real changes.
    b. the adverse effects of a higher minimum wage are quite substantial.
    c. a higher minimum wage helps small firms and businesses.
    d. a higher minimum wage results in an increase in employment and the economy in general.

___5. Critics of the minimum wage argue that

    a. it makes firms less willing to train workers lacking basic skills.
    b. it encourages companies to hire more low-skilled workers.
    c. firms become more generous with fringe benefits when the minimum wage is increased.
    d. the minimum wage usually results in less discrimination.

Chapter 16: Public Policy/Contemporary Issues
Selection 17: When Living Is a Fate Worse Than Death

Reading Level 7.5

Introduction

- Remind students about the tips for studying philosophy and ethics: Read critically; look for reasons that support a position; consider opposing viewpoints.
- Ask students the following: How does our view of death affect our view of life? How does our view of life affect how we face death? Is false hope better than no hope at all? Explain that, again, they will be reading a story about a moral dilemma. Frequently with ethics, there are no absolutes and the gray areas can make us struggle the most—especially when the suffering of an infant is involved.

Follow-Up

- If you were a counselor, what could you have done to help Charlotte's parents deal realistically with the situation and prepare for their infant's death?
- Mention the "Living Funeral" which Morrie planned for himself in *Tuesdays with Morrie*. (Albom, M. *Tuesdays with Morrie,* Doubleday 1997, pp. 12-13)
- After students have previewed and read, ask them to brainstorm ideas for the table on the next page.

Summary

Who: Charlotte
What: Was the subject of a controversy between parents, medical ethicists, and doctors
When: Recently
Where:
Why: Born with a debilitating, life-threatening brain abnormality
How: Medical advancements offered a slightly prolonged, albeit painful, life through operations and feeding tubes

Sample:

Recently in the , infant Charlotte was the subject of a moral controversy between parents, medical ethicists, and doctors. Born with a debilitating, life-threatening brain abnormality, she was offered a slightly prolonged, albeit painful, life through medically advanced operations and the use of a feeding tube.

Pro: Allow Charlotte to Die	Con: Attempt All Measures to Prolong Life
Reasons:	Reasons:

Support?   Support?

Who should make these decisions? Parents? Doctors? Laws?
Should the government be allowed to enter the decision-making process?
How can parents better cope with difficult decisions?

Quiz: When Living Is a Fate Worse Than Death

True/False

___1. Charlotte's parents had unrealistic expectations of doctors' medical abilities in the
.

___2. Because they are from Haiti, Charlotte's parents were actually skeptical and superstitious of American medicine.

___3. Hospitals dislike ethicists because they always side in favor of prolonging the patient's life.

Multiple Choice

___4. In Charlotte's case, the hospital's Ethics Advisory Committee considered all of the following issues *except*

      a. parents' rights supersede the caregiver's beliefs about what is right.
      b. painful procedures should be avoided.
      c. all measures to prolong and sustain life are warranted, no matter what the expected outcome and no matter what the intensity of pain endured by the patient.
      d. the care that Charlotte's parents wanted for her should be provided unless there was a medical consensus that it would not prolong her life.

___5. The possible explanations for why the hospital staff did not save Charlotte from a horrible death included all of the following *except*

      a. the possibility of death was not seriously considered.
      b. they feared the parents would take them to court, as in the case of the mother in Virginia who got a judge to order the hospital to provide treatment for her anencephalic baby.
      c. they feared being dragged into the media spotlight, as was the staff at a Pennsylvania hospital who withdrew life support, against the parents' wishes, from a comatose three-year-old with fatal brain cancer.
      d. they were wrong.

Reading Level: 5

Introduction

- Ask students what compels adoptees to seek out birth parents, especially when they know that their parents willingly gave them up.
- Ask students if they can think of stories in literature in which characters sought to find their birth parents or other ancestors.
- Make a copy of the Anticipation Guide on the next page. Ask students to respond to the six statements before reading the selection. They may find it difficult to decide but request that they chose an answer.

Follow-Up

- Ask students to complete the time-line from the text. Use the handout on page 126 as a transparency to discuss the sequence with the class.
- Refer back to the Anticipation Guide. Again ask students to respond to the statements. Discuss their reasons for changing any answers. Did anything in this article prompt them to think differently? What is the benefit of reading about the experience of others?

Summary

Who:	Rick Reilly
What:	Recounts the journey to locate and meet his adopted daughter's birth mother
When:	When Rae is 11 and asking about her mother
Where:	Travel to Korea
Why:	Rae is restless to fill a hole in her heart
How:	Effective sleuthing by Friends of Children of Various Nations, an organization which arranges a trip to Korea.

Sample:

Journalist Rick Reilly recounts his family's journey to locate and meet his adopted daughter's Korean birth mother. Because 11-year-old Rae is curious and eager to fill an emptiness in her heart, her adopted family is successfully aided by effective sleuthing from Friends of Children of Various Nations, an organization which arranges the trip to Korea.

Anticipation Guide

Response Before Reading	Statement	Response After Reading
(agree/disagree)	Adopted children should not seek out their birth parents—it can cause too much pain and heartache.	(agree/disagree)
	It is not fair to the parents of adopted children, if those children try to find his or her birth parents.	
	Mothers who give away babies probably spend their lives regretting the decision.	
	Adoptive parents cannot love a child as much as the real birth parents.	
	Adopted children probably always feel a little isolated.	
	Society blames mothers who give babies up for adoption.	

Time Line for Seoul Searching

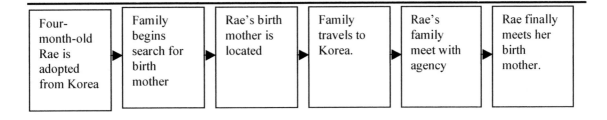

Four-month-old Rae is adopted from Korea → Family begins search for birth mother → Rae's birth mother is located → Family travels to Korea. → Rae's family meet with agency → Rae finally meets her birth mother.

Quiz: Seoul Searching

True/False

____1. Rae was often self-conscious and felt that people stared at her because she looked different.

____2. Rae's mother gave her up for adoption because at the time of Rae's birth she was married to a man who was not Rae's father.

____3. For Rae's mother, giving Rae up for adoption was especially difficult because the baby was the product of a long, loving relationship with a childhood sweetheart, but she had to marry the man who was selected by her family.

Multiple Choice

____4. When contact with Rae's birth mother was established, the meeting took place

        a. in the van parked outside the town's boundaries.
        b. in a coffee shop in a neighboring town.
        c. in a park.
        d. at the adoption agency.

____5. Rae's reaction at having met her birth mother can best be described as

        a. disappointment at the iciness of her birth mother.
        a. despair over having to leave her, knowing there would never again be any contact.
        c. jealousy over her birth mother's other children.
        d. elation at having her questions answered and the hole in her heart healed.

Reading Level: 9

Introduction

- Ask your students if anyone in the classroom has ever been a victim of political oppression. Do they know of anyone persecuted for political or religious reasons? What do they know about the Holocaust? What kinds of problems do refugees encounter when they emigrate to foreign countries?
- Bring in an overhead of a world map. Ask your students to find Iraq. Discuss the reality of living conditions for women under the Taliban, in Saudi Arabia, and in Afghanistan under strict interpretations of Islamic rule. Explain what a *burqa* is, and ask them to imagine walking in the heat completely covered in the shroud-like veil, or being arrested for displaying an ankle.
- Finally, bring in a copy of *Zoya's Story*: *An Afghan Woman's Battle for Freedom* by Zoya with John Follain and Rita Cristofari. This novel relates the memoirs of a girl whose parents are killed by Muslim fundamentalists when she is 14. Zoya reveals no details of how her parents were killed out of fear that her identity will be discovered. (*The Kite Runner* by Khaled Hosseini is another timely novel based around Afghanistan from a boy's point of view.) Invite students to read either of these books for extra credit.

Follow-Up

- After students have previewed and read the selection, ask them to work in groups to complete the notes on the next page. Assign each group a stage to complete, then share their work.

Summary

Who: A Kurdish family of six sisters
What: Fled their homeland, undergoing horrific living conditions and experiences
When: In the 1980s
Where: From Iraq, to Pakistan, to Iran, to America.
Why: When Sadam Hussein came into power, their lives were in danger.
How: Walked on foot

Sample:

After Sadam Hussein came into power in the 1980s, a Kurdish family of six girls fled for their lives, walking on foot to Pakistan, then on to Iran, where they lived under horrific conditions for ten years before finally emigrating to America.

Significant Events Taking Place in Each Stage of the Journey

Baghdad	Iran (Refugee Camp) 1 year	Pakistan (Quetta) 10 years	Pakistan Islamabad (1 year)	America Lincoln, Nebraska

Quiz: The Beautiful Laughing Sisters—An Arrival Story

True/False

_____1. Once this Kurdish family escaped from Baghdad, they felt much safer.

_____2. The girls were forced to cover themselves with hot, heavy robes during their time spent in Quetta.

_____3. It took little time for the family to emigrate to America once they arrived at the refugee camp.

Multiple Choice

_____4. After fleeing their native country, all of the following happened *except*

    a. the sisters betrayed their parents in exchange for food and passage to America.
    b. the girls were chased and harassed.
    c. the family walked three days without food and little water.
    d. the family went on a hunger strike.

_____5. With which statement below would the author most likely agree?

    a. Police everywhere see their main priority as offering protection to innocent people.
    b. Refugee camps are a good temporary solution for families of political exiles.
    c. Single women have few privileges or protection in some places.
    d. American life is very similar to life in other countries.

Reading Level: 16

Introduction

- Remind students of the tips for studying political science/government/history: Focus on the significant events, both current and historical; analyze motivation/consider political organization; be alert for bias and partisanship; sort facts from opinions.
- Prior to assigning the selection, write the three categories of terrorists on the board and have students brainstorm what they know. Use the KWL format on the next page.
- Remind students about the cues in textbooks that signal important terms or concepts. Instruct students to pay attention to these cues as they preview and read.
- After previewing, students will fill in what they want to know.
- After reading, they will fill in what they have learned.

Follow-Up

- After completing the KWL chart, have students complete the map in the text.
- Ask if the article contains only facts, or if opinions are also present.
- Walk the students through the following critical thinking questions. You may want to divide the questions among small groups of students and ask them to work out the answers. Circulate around the room and offer some clues if students do not understand the question.

Critical Thinking

1. State the purpose of the article clearly.
2. What is the question the author is attempting to settle?
3. What assumptions is the author making?
4. What is the author's point of view?
5. How are the author's claims supported? What data, information, or evidence does the author provide?
6. Identify the key concepts
7. What conclusions does the author draw?
8. What are the implications or consequences suggested by the article?

- Create a "Research Riddle Assignment." Ask students to research infamous figures or groups who could be classified as terrorists from current politics or history, either living or dead. Using library and Internet sources, they will provide eight clues about their person. They should number their clues 1-8, providing the most difficult first and leading to the easiest. Ask them to use at least three sources, citing each as a reference.

What You **K**now	What You **W**ant to Know	What You **L**earned

Quiz: Profile of a Terrorist

True/False

____1. The author believes that it is possible to predict the behavior of some terrorists.

____2. The category "*crazies*" is assigned to people whose motives are easily understood.

____3. According to Frederick Hacker, *crusaders* appear to be normal people.

Multiple Choice

____4. According to this selection, the majority of people who commit modern terrorism fall into the category of

      a. crazies.
      b. criminals.
      c. crusaders.
      d. both a and c.

____5. One major difference between a *crusader* and a terrorist of the other two categories is

      a. a *crusader* is motivated mostly by profit.
      b. a *crusader* is the least likely to negotiate a resolution.
      c. a *crusader* can be easily swayed to resolve an issue.
      d. a *crusader's* behavior is easily predictable.

Reading Level: 11

Introduction

- Ask students if they feel included in the political process in the .
  If not, inquire why they feel they are being excluded. What suggestions do they have that would make the political system more relevant?
- Next, ask students what they know about the history of voting in the America. Write the term *suffrage* on the board and mention briefly the struggle that many groups of people underwent to earn this right.
- Bring in a copy of *Animal Farm* by George Orwell. (This is an excellent opportunity to discuss the elements of satire.) Explain how the animals, led by the pigs, revolted against their human masters and decided to run the farm themselves. All the animals had equal privileges, but some animals quickly became "more equal" than others. Eventually, the pigs became corrupted by power and a new tyranny was established. Invite students to read this novel for extra credit.

Follow-Up

- After students have previewed and read the selection, ask them to close their textbooks and share one fact that is most memorable. Write these on the board to determine which ones made the most impression. Then ask the students to give additional facts which they remember. Finally, have students open their texts to verify the accuracy of what they could remember. Then ask students to locate common ideas, using circles, boxes, and underlining to designate common points. Divide students into groups and assign each group the task of composing a map of major and minor points for each grouping. Ask the groups to work on simplifying their ideas and then combining the maps on the board in order to create a graphic organizer of notes from this selection.
- Instruct students to circle words in the selection that signal a list of reasons and a list of contrasting ideas.
- Make a transparency of the next page which traces the history of voting in the . Ask students to analyze the list and draw some conclusions about barriers that were put into place in order to restrict voting privileges for different groups of people. What can they infer from these descriptions?

History of Voting

1776 When this country announced its independence from Britain, voting rights were based on property ownership. This typically meant that those voting were white males over the age of 21 and of the Protestant faith.

1787 In the newly drafted Constitution, states were given the power to set voting mandates and most were still favorable to white males who owned property.

1830 Many states had dropped religion and property ownership as requirements for voting and, with such a large percentage of the population at the polls, political parties were beginning to develop.

1868 The 14th Amendment recognized African Americans as citizens, giving them the right to vote. However, state officials continued attempts to deny this right.

1870 African Americans were given the right to vote in the 15th Amendment. It prohibited any state or local government from denying that right.

1890 Wyoming became the first state to recognize women's right to vote and provide for it in a state constitution.

1913 Voting power was expanded with the 17th Amendment, calling for the popular election of U. S. senators.

1920 The 19th Amendment was added to the Constitution, giving women across the nation the right to vote.

1940 Congress recognized Native Americans as citizens. However, it wasn't until 1947 that all states granted them the right to vote.

1964 The 24th Amendment declared that no person should be denied the right to vote because he or she cannot pay a "poll tax."

1965 An amendment to the Voting Rights Act banned the use of literacy tests, poll taxes, and other obstacles designed to keep people from voting.

1971 The voting age was lowered to 18.

*Source: http://www.flaglerelections.com/   (Oct. 4, 2006)

Quiz: Whether to Vote: A Citizen's First Choice

True/False

___ 1. Citizens of the tend to have a better voting turnout than do citizens of other countries.

___ 2. The chance of one vote's affecting the outcome of a presidential election is very slight.

___ 3. citizens can now vote by email in national and state elections.

Multiple Choice

___ 4. All of the following were given as a reason for low voter turnout *except*

    a. voter registration.
    b. frequency of voting.
    c. large number of political offices.
    d. great disparity among political parties.

___ 5. In the , as the right to vote spread to include a greater variety of people, the number of citizens voting

    a. tended to decrease proportionately.
    b. tended to increase proportionately.
    c. stayed the same.
    d. jumped dramatically.

Reading Level: 7

Introduction

- Give all students an index card and have them write their answer to the following question which, at one time, was a question on the admissions application for Dartmouth College:

  "Describe yourself in ten years from the viewpoint of a close friend."

- Locate a copy of Maria Shriver's *Ten Things I Wish I'd Known Before I Went Out into the Real World* and share the list.
- Relate Ben Carson's story of one unusual circumstance that led to his landing a position at Johns Hopkins Hospital. As a young man, Carson had decided to familiarize himself with classical music. It just so happened that the doctor who interviewed him was a classical music buff and an immediate a bond was formed between the two men. Invite students to read *Gifted Hands* or *Think Big* for extra credit.
- Ask the students if a life of rich and varied experiences provides rich and varied opportunities.

Follow-Up

- Have students make a list of things they love to do on the back of their index card, on the left-hand side and jobs that might correspond to the list:

Do What You Love

What You Love to Do	Job Possibilities

Quiz: Four Simple Words That Guarantee the Job of Your Dreams

True/False

___1. The author Martha Finney has worked as a sailing instructor for the past five years because of her love of the sport and the opportunities where she lives.

___2. The author recommends quitting your present job to go in search of something else.

___3. The author recommends finding a job that dovetails with your passion so that your passion becomes your job.

Multiple Choice

___4. The author has worked as a

    a. writer for *Ally McBeal*.
    b. receptionist for a Manhattan public-relations firm.
    c. aailing instructor.
    d. writer for *The Twilight Zone*.

___5. The author would agree with all of the following *except*

    a. Research a company and primarily negotiate for good benefits, including stock options.
    b. Research jobs available in your field of interest.
    c. The strategy of being at the right place at the right time often results from doing what you love.
    d. Spend time in an environment that fascinates you and seek a job that is available there.

Reading Level: 13

Introduction

- Remind students of the tips for studying business/advertising/economics: Focus on the process; focus on the theme of globalization; consider ethical decision-making and social responsibility.
- Review the list of emotional words in the text, and ask students when a writer might use emotional words in his or her writing.
- Have the students create a list of emotional words which PETA, People for the Ethical Treatment of Animals, might use to manipulate public opinion and encourage consumers to become vegetarians.

Follow-Up

- Ask the students to point out emotional words used in the article.
- Ask the students to locate spelling, grammatical, and stylistic errors that may detract from the credibility of the site and, therefore, may indicate a need for further investigation to verify the facts.

Summary

Who: McDonald's
What: Is accused of practices that anger the public
When: Presently
Where: Worldwide
Why: For a profit
How: Alleged exploitation of animals, the environment, and workers

Sample:

Presently, some people are angry at the alleged exploitative business policies and practices that McDonald's exercises to ensure a profit at the expense of the environment, and the rights of its workers and animals.

Quiz: McDonald's Makes a Lot of People Angry for a Lot of Different Reasons

True/False

____1. The Web site, McSpotlight, could be characterized as anti-McDonald's with an apparent bias against the fast-food chain.

____2. McDonald's has spent a fortune on marketing practices to present itself as environmentally friendly.

____3. It has been proven in court lawsuits that McDonald's is responsible for the destruction of tropical forests.

Multiple Choice

____4. The creators of this Web site would agree with all of the following *except*

        a. McDonald's employs more than a million mostly young people worldwide.
        b. McDonald's helps reduce the unemployment rate.
        c. McDonald's is a destroyer of jobs.
        d. McDonald's exploits young workers.

____5. The authors use emotional words to depict the McDonald's Corporation as

        a. altruistic and unselfish.
        b. arrogant and self-serving.
        c. congenial and environmentally friendly.
        d. a promoter of free speech and human rights.

Reading Level: 12

Introduction

- Begin by explaining that advertisers develop strategies for effective marketing. One strategy is to combine the emotions of pleasure and pain with their product, so that consumers associate pleasure with the product that appears to alleviate or even eliminate pain. An example is the TV ad by the people of Philip Morris (makers of cigarettes) who sent representatives to Bosnia to deliver food, clothing, and medical supplies as an international goodwill gesture. Another popular tactic is to display products or their logos in movies aimed at particular age groups. For example, the films *Gone in 60 Seconds* and *Fast and Furious* are replete with car products, and their targeted audience is a youthful, diverse culture of people fascinated with cars. Likewise, this selection is about marketing strategies targeting a new audience.
- If you can locate any advertising that is focused on Hispanics, either magazine ads or a TV commercial, the example would provide a good "set" for the students prior to previewing and reading Selection 24.
- Describe a current advertisement that is particularly memorable. What makes it stand out? At whom is the ad aimed?

Follow-Up

- Ask students about what kind of ethics do they think advertisers, who are in the business of manipulating thinking, might have.
- Is there a difference between political propaganda and advertising?

Summary

Who: Advertisers
What: Focus on young Hispanic-American population
Where: In areas in the with growing numbers of Hispanic Americans
When: Presently
Why: Lucrative opportunities with the rising Hispanic population
How: Geographic concentration, understanding Hispanic identity, product loyalty, and increased spending power

Sample:
Presently in the , advertisers are marketing products in certain areas of the country toward the growing Hispanic-American population through geographic concentration, an understanding of Hispanic identity, product loyalty, and increased spending power.

Quiz: Hispanic Americans: A Growing Market Segment

True/False

___1. The median age of Hispanic Americans is 32.6, while the United States average is 23.6.

___2. The Hispanic family tends to be much smaller than the rest of the families in the country.

___3. Hispanics tend to be brand-loyal.

Multiple Choice

___4. One main reason the Hispanic market is being explored and subsequently cultivated is because

      a. they tend not to be loyal to one brand, so the challenge is there for many companies.
      b. they tend to be very spread out, and advertisers have a lot of territory, geographically, to share with competitors.
      c. the education level is increasing; therefore, the spending power increases.
      d. all Americans like Hispanic influence in their advertising.

___5. If you worked for an advertising agency that aspired to develop a rapport with Hispanic Americans, you would most likely purchase air time for your ad on

      a. ethnic soap operas.
      b. ice hockey games.
      c. cooking shows featuring the preparation of exotic dishes such as salmon and Béarnaise sauce.
      d. a documentary on the history of Jazz.

Reading Level: 14

Introduction

- Remind students about the tips for studying technology/computer courses: Read slowly; notice technical vocabulary; focus on process; use visualization.
- Discuss work-place ethics with regard to computer usage. How do employers feel about students' using computers for personal business? What are the privacy issues concerning email? Can students think of any kind of work information that shouldn't be included in personal emails?
- Define the term *blogging* and bring in an example of a current blog to read to the class. Inform students that blogging has become established as a key part of online culture. Ask if there are any bloggers in the class. Next, ask students why they presently use the Internet to compose Web logs. Who is the audience? Have any problems ensued as a result? Can students envision any dangers associated with blogging? Explain that as they preview this selection, they will discover that some serious issues have arisen as a result of blogs.

Follow-Up

- Have students brainstorm what they can recall, and then ask them to organize those ideas according to the map in the text under "Reviewing and Organizing Ideas" on page 441.

Summary

Who: Bloggers
What: The legal difficulties and penalities that bloggers face
When: Currently
Where: Worldwide
Why: To make bloggers aware of the potential problems
How: Through blogs about the workplace that can be considered defamatory or that reveal proprietary information

Sample:

Currently, bloggers are facing penalties and legal difficulties for including information in their blogs that companies consider proprietary or defamatory.

Quiz: Blogger Beware

True/False

___1. Proprietary information is confidential information that is considered the property of a company.

___2. The release of proprietary information in a blog could be grounds for punishment by a company.

___3. Comments in blogs that promote union activities or other social activities will most likely cause a worker to lose his or her job.

Multiple Choice

___4. Companies have every right to regulate blogging and other computer activity if

    a. employees are blogging on company time or endangering network security.
    b. employees are grousing that night about the bad work day they had.
    c. employees are complaining about government issues on their lunch hour.
    d. the company is dissatisfied with the employee's performance and is looking for a way to fire that employee based upon his or her after-hours blogs.

___5. Making false statements about a person that damage the person's reputation or deter others from associating with that person is known as

    a. defamation.
    b. proprietary information.
    c. whistle-blogging.
    d. trade secrets.

Reading Level: 10

Introduction

- Ask students to consider how ethical concerns have increased along with the growth of technology. Can students cite any examples of new technology that has been used in harmful ways?
- Write the words "privacy abuse" on the board. Ask students to think of examples that might be considered privacy abuse. Take a poll of the class to learn how many students own camera phones. Can students think of instances where the use of camera phones could be considered abusive?
- Make two columns on the board, labeling one "Pro-Camera Phones" and "Anti-Camera Phones." Circle the room asking students to mention supportive reasons or evidence for each side. Before reading this selection, ask students to decide with a show of hands which side they support. Write the numbers on the board.

Follow-Up

- Ask students to discuss how camera phones can be detrimental. What privacy issues does the selection mention? List the problems on the board. Then direct students to find the solutions that were suggested. Do students think these solutions are effective measures? Can they think of any others?

- Now take a revote about the issue of camera-phone pictures. Did students change their minds? If so, why?

Summary

Who: Cell phone users
What: Violating privacy by taking inappropriate pictures of unsuspecting citizens privacy.
When: Currently
Where: In public places
Why: Secretive
How: With camera phones

Sample:

Currently, cell phones with cameras have been used to secretly take inappropriate pictures of unsuspecting citizens in public places, violating their right to privacy.

Quiz: Hold It Right There, and Drop That Camera

True/False

___1. The American Civil Liberties Union is an organization that works to protect the rights of industry.

___2. According to the article, enforcing the regulation of camera-phone use is a fairly easy task.

___3. According to the author, citizens have the right to privacy in public places such as bathrooms and locker rooms.

Multiple Choice

___4. While some people consider the benefits of camera phones, others complain that

        a. they are being used in commercials.
        b. they are being used inappropriately.
        c. they are transmitting pictures instantly.
        d. camera phones are becoming more numerous.

___5. Elk Grove Park District is enacting a ban on cell-phone transgressions by

        a. searching bags in locker room areas.
        b. monitoring cell-phone use.
        c. arresting people who use their cell phones to make calls in public changing rooms.
        d. expecting people to voluntarily comply.

Reading Level: 11

Introduction

- Ask if any students in the class plan to study criminal justice. Next, ask if anyone is aware of new technology currently being used or developed in the field of criminal justice.
- Write the title of the selection on the board and have students predict what they will read about before previewing.

Follow-Up

- Have students brainstorm what they recall. Write these ideas on the board, giving each student an opportunity for input. Then have them open their text and verify their answers.
- Solicit opinions on electronic monitoring. Is it humiliating? Is it actually better than incarceration? Does it endanger other members of a community? How safe would you feel if you lived next door to someone who is being monitored electronically?

Summary

Who: Trend in law enforcement
What: Electronic monitoring provides inexpensive option for keeping track of nonviolent offenders
When: Currently
Where:
Why: Allows them to be at home with their families
How: Electronic transmitter—as long as offenders comply with rules

Sample:

Currently in the United States, electronic monitoring, a new trend in law enforcement, provides an inexpensive option for keeping track of nonviolent offenders by allowing them to be at home with their families as long as they wear the transmitter and comply with the court's rules.

Quiz: House Arrest and Electronic Monitoring

True/False

___1. Offenders under house arrest are not allowed to have jobs.

___2. Except for being confined to their homes, offenders under house arrest are not required to follow any other rules.

___3. The offender wears an unremovable ankle band holding a transmitter that sends a signal to the receiver.

Multiple Choice

___4. With which statement below about electronic monitoring would the authors disagree?

    a. Electronic monitoring is low-cost.
    b. Most participants appreciate the opportunity to be near loved ones.
    c. It prevents offenders from committing domestic crimes.
    d. Only nonviolent criminal offenders are allowed to participate in electronic monitoring.

___5. All of the statements about electronic monitoring are true *except*

    a. It protects society.
    b. It keeps offenders out of the workplace and prevents them from improving their future prospects.
    c. It punishes offenders.
    d. It reduces prison overcrowding and correctional costs.

Reading Level: 9

Introduction

- Remind students of the tips for studying health-related fields: Learn the necessary terminology; learn about the basic human body systems; read critically.
- Point out the food pyramid on page 471 of the text and survey how many students in the class actually adhere to it.
- Acquaint students with the U.S. Department of Agriculture Web site—www.mypyramid.gov. Students can use this resource to track their own diets, obtain a customized food guide, and learn more about making smart choices.
- Make a transparency of the KWL chart on the board similar to the one on the next page. Have students brainstorm what they already *know* about nutrition, exercise, and weight loss. Next, in the second column, have them list some things they *want to know*. In the last column, you will have them write what they have learned after reading the article.

Follow-Up

- After completing the preview and reading, have students complete the last column of the KWL chart.
- Divide the class into groups to collaboratively complete the diagram on page 478 of the text. Make copies of the chart on the following page. Ask students to keep a journal for a week about their diets and exercise.

Summary

Who: Marilee Arthur, a plus-size fitness trainer
What: Receives some training and advice on weight loss
When: Recently
Where: Plattsville, Ontario
Why: Because she wanted to feel more energetic and to increase her strength
How: By changing her diet—particularly when and what she eats—and changing her exercise routine

Sample:

Recently, Plattsville, Ontario, native and plus-size fitness trainer Marilee Arthur received some training and expert weight-loss advice. Because she wanted to feel more energetic and to increase her strength, she changed what and when she ate, as well as her exercise routine, in order to get the maximum benefits of both.

What You Know	What You Want to Know	What You Have Learned

Food Pyramid

	Grains	Vegetables	Fruits	Milk	Meat and Beans	Physical Activity
Breakfast						
Lunch						
Dinner						
Snacks						

How did you do yesterday? _____

What is your goal for tomorrow? _____

Quiz: Use It and Lose It

True/False

____1. It is not starch but the quantity of starch that can increase body fat.

____2. Fruits and vegetables can provide the carbohydrates needed for energy as well as fiber.

____3. Varying one's eating routine and eating at different times each day will help with weight loss.

Multiple Choice

____4. According to the article, the best time of day to work out in order to lose weight is

      a. in the morning, because it burns fat.
      b. in early afternoon, because you have more energy to burn fat.
      c. during the late afternoon, because it prevents pulled muscles.
      d. after dinner, to burn the calories of the day.

____5. When lifting weights to increase muscle, you should

      a. increase weight and decrease the repetitions.
      b. decrease weight and increase the repetitions.
      c. maintain the same weight and repetitions.
      d. never do so much weight that the muscle fibers tear microscopically.

Reading Level: 15

Introduction

- Write the word *vigilant* on the board and discuss predictions about what it may have to do with the medical profession.
- Ask students the following: How would you feel if you went into the hospital for knee surgery and came out of the operating room only to find the orthopedist had operated on the wrong knee? Or what would you do if the pharmacist misread the doctor's handwriting and filled your prescription incorrectly?
- How important is it that you be informed about your illness and possible treatments, as well as side effects? Do you rely on the doctor for all of your information? What questions do you ask?

Follow-Up

- Ask students to complete the conceptual map on the next page in order to consider ways to become vigilant about their health care. Refer them to the section " To Improve Is Human" on page 488 of their text.

Summary

Who: Critics
What: Warn about mistakes in medical treatments and drug prescriptions
When: Currently
Where: Medical community
Why: Human error
How: Patients can avoid effects of the mistakes by being vigilant

Sample:

Critics warn that mistakes in medical treatments and drug prescriptions can pose risks because of human error; therefore, patients should be vigilant through proper communication and personal research.

Ways to Improve Your Personal Health Care through Consumer Education

Understanding your treatment

?

Keeping organized records of the medicines you take

?

Quiz: Make No Mistake: Medical Errors Can Be Deadly Serious

True/False

___1. More people die each year from automobile accidents than from medical mistakes.

___2. The FDA works with pharmacy companies in naming drugs to prevent possible confusion.

___3. Though not perfect, electronic systems for prescriptions can help prevent mistakes.

Multiple Choice

___4. With which statement below would the author disagree?

    a. Name confusion is among the most common causes of drug-related errors.
    b. The use of bar codes on prescriptions prevents any errors.
    c. A person would have to fly nonstop for 438 years before expecting to be involved in a deadly airplane crash.
    d. Computer science can fail, too.

___5. Despite technological advances, preventing medical mistakes will depend on

    a. government funding of medical research.
    b. government regulations of insurance companies.
    c. care and watchfulness of health professionals and patients.
    d. better computer systems.

Reading Level: 16

Introduction

- When you hear the word *steroid*, does it have a positive or negative connotation? Explain your answer.
- Are all steroids bad, or do some have positive medical effects?
- Locate an advertisement for a performance-enhancing drug and ask students if they can detect any biased language.
- Tell students that the 1976 International Olympic Committee banned the use of steroids by athletes and began requiring urine tests. What is their opinion?
- In the 1988 Summer Olympics, track star Ben Johnson's medal was rescinded when it was discovered that he had used Stanozolol. What is their opinion?

Follow-Up

- After students have previewed and read the passage, remind them that they should pay attention to new terminology when reading about health-related issues. Since this article is at a high reading level, ask the student if there is any terminology that needs to be clarified.
- Use the conceptual map on page 155 of the manual to discuss the two columns which students created in their notes on the benefits and risks of steroid use. Remind students of the cause-and-effect organizational pattern.

Summary

Who: Athletes
What: Use of anabolic steroids and performance-enhancing drugs
When: Currently
Where: Worldwide
Why: To increase muscle tissue and enhance appearance
How: Illegally sold drugs as well as over-the-counter performance-enhancing drugs which are not FDA-regulated

Sample:

A current worldwide trend among athletes, particularly body-builders, to use anabolic steroids and performance-enhancing drugs for increasing muscles and enhancing appearance can have negative long-term effects and is creating concern since these drugs are not FDA-regulated.

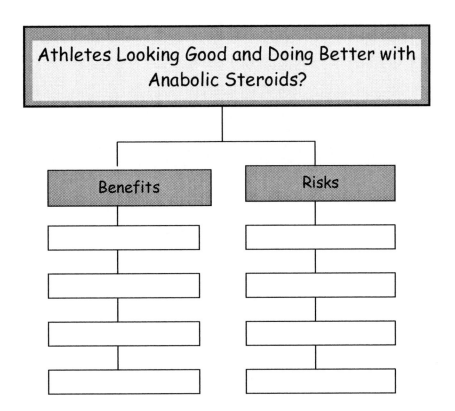

Quiz: Athletes Looking Good and Doing Better
with Anabolic Steroids?

True/False

____1. Steroid use has been banned in the United States since the 1960s.

____2. While Olympic athletes are not allowed to use steroids, they are allowed to use over-the-counter drugs, such as FDA-regulated cold medicines.

____3. It is suspected that professional body-builders are frequent users of anabolic steroids.

Multiple Choice

____4. A nutritional performance-enhancer is a

  a. euphemism for androstenedione, which is converted to testosterone in the body.
  b. natural way to provide the body with nutrients which are often unwittingly expelled from the body.
  c. healthful way to ensure the efficacy of nutrients in natural foods.
  d. healthful power shake created by a physical trainer and physician of the United States Olympic Swim Team.

____5. The term *'roid rage* refers to the

  a. sudden surge of physical power gained overnight with brief steroid use.
  b. brand name of a performance-enhancer used by Mark McGwire.
  c. violent behavior exhibited by steroid users.
  d. derogatory name given to the FDA by makers of anabolic steroids.

Reading Level: 11

Introduction

- Ask how many students have a pet dog. Ask them to describe the motions their dogs exhibit when greeting another dog and initiating play. Describe the "play bow" and ask if they have noticed this.

- Have students follow along as you read aloud the first paragraph of the selection. Ask them to make predictions about the contents of the selection. What do they already know about animal behavior? What do they expect to learn from this article?

- Introduce students to the history of Charles Darwin, who was perhaps the first animal ethnologist. Explain that Darwin observed animals in their natural habitats and stressed the hereditary contributions to animal behavior. He became internationally famous for his theories of evolution and had a tremendous impact on religious thought. It is interesting to note that Darwin was described as a slow learner while in school. In his autobiography, Darwin relays the story of his father's removing him from school at the age of sixteen because he was not paying attention to his studies, was getting poor grades, and was excessive lazy. It is ironic to think that his father declared to him that he "cared for nothing but shooting, dogs, and rat-catching, and you will be a disgrace to yourself and all your family." Darwin left school as an entirely unremarkable student, and none of his instructors thought he possessed any noteworthy abilities. Invite students to read about Charles Darwin on the Internet and bring in information about his life and/or theories.

Follow-Up

- Ask students their opinion of the statement about Jaak Panskepp from the article: "He is sure that rats and other animals do experience joy, sadness, anger, and fear—because the wiring of the brain is set up to generate those feelings."

- Instruct students to fill in the conceptual map on page 509 under the section Reviewing and Organizing Ideas: Mapping.

- Using critical reading skills and considering the language used in this selection, ask students to point out words that help the reader decide if the statements about animal behavior are facts, opinions, or theories. What is the difference? Remind them that facts in a scientific context are a generally accepted reality (but still open to scientific inquiry, as opposed to an absolute truth.) Hypotheses and theories are generally based on objective inferences, unlike opinions, which are generally based on subjective beliefs. Ask students to fill in the chart on the next page.

Fact or Theory?

Statement	Evidence
Dogs exchange information as they play.	
Animals have emotions.	
Animals can be envious.	
Animals can have empathy.	
Animals can express altruism.	
Animals have a sense of fairness.	
Animals have strict rules of behavior.	
Animals have a sense of morality.	

Quiz: Honor Among Beasts

True/False

___1. This article suggests that some animals have a rudimentary version of morality.

___2. Scientists have observed capuchin monkeys sharing food when they could have eaten it by themselves.

___3. Scientists agree that the concepts of fairness and justice exist only in a few animals such as dolphins, dogs, and primates, but not in other animals such as rats or birds.

Multiple Choice

___4. The authors would probably agree with all of the following statements *except*

    a. Dogs use physical gestures to signal their intentions to other dogs.
    b. Animals are capable of emotion.
    c. Moral behavior is limited to the human race.
    d. Some animals exhibit a sense of justice.

___5. Strict rules of behavior have been observed in

    a. cockroaches, ants, and beetles.
    b. fish and sea life.
    c. dogs, rats, and birds.
    d. all animals, all birds, and all insects.

Reading Level: 13

Introduction

- If you can make transparencies of the photographs of the pillow bugs, the enlarged pictures would be a dramatic introduction.
- After showing the picture, ask the students what kind of creature and habitat would they expect to read about.
- Write the word *microcarnivores* and ask for ideas of its meaning. Point out that *micro=small; carn=flesh; vores=eaters.*
- Finally, tell the students that these creatures are pillow mites and ask for some predictions about what the article will explain. Write these on the board.

Follow-Up

- Ask each student which fact was most memorable. Write the answers on the board.
- Ask students to evaluate the author's style. Is the tone severe, panicked, grave, or pessimistic? Is the article, instead, written with some levity? Is it possible to write a scientific article with a light-hearted tone? Ask students for some examples of humorous imagery.

Summary

Who:	Pillow mites
What:	May be responsible for high levels of asthma in some parts of the country
When:	Constantly
Where:	Present in even the most hygienic of situations
Why:	Microscopic
How:	Breed quickly and feed off dead skin

Sample:

Pillow mites, though microscopic, are present in even the most hygienic situations; however, in large numbers they may be responsible for high rates of asthma in areas of the country where specific conditions are conducive to breeding.

Quiz: Bugs in Your Pillow

True/False

____1. There is a correlation between asthma and pillow mites.

____2. Areas such as Tennessee and Maryland have the lowest levels of mites and therefore the lowest levels of asthma.

____3. Fluffing pillows routinely will help reduce the growth of mites.

Multiple Choice

____4. Despite their name and appearance, Dermatophagoides, the flesh-eating mites, are

        a. really quite mild.
        b. more treacherous than originally determined.
        c. necessary to humans to promote circulation on the scalp.
        d. in danger of becoming extinct.

____5. Pillow mites could be less of a problem if homeowners

        a. washed and boiled pillows regularly.
        b. slept without pillows.
        c. allowed pets near pillows to entice the transfer to pet fur.
        d. routinely fluffed pillows outside.

Reading Level: 16

Introduction

- Begin by sharing a transparency of the memo on the next page in which Jacqueline Spencer, Assistant Professor of Biology at Thomas Nelson Community College, stresses the importance of learning the vocabulary when studying biology.
- Ask the students to follow along as you read aloud the first sentence in the text, page 531. Ask the students what a *biodiversity crisis* means. Next, ask them to explain the phrase "precipitous decline in the Earth's great variety of life."
- Have the students predict species that the article may cite as being in jeopardy.
- Tell the students about the years of DDT use which caused the shells of bald eagles to become so fragile that they were transparent. Consequently, the babies died before they could hatch. Therefore, the use of DDT was banned and eagles are now more plentiful.
- Ask them about this comment from meteorologist and North Carolina State University professor Dr. Michael Kaplan, who, when asked if the Earth is in danger of being destroyed, replied, "The Earth will be fine. It has always had the ability to heal itself. The *Earth* will be fine." While it seems like good news, what is the implication about human life?

Follow-Up

- To accommodate visual learners, have the students complete the outline on page 538 of the text and then transfer the information to a conceptual map on page 164 of the manual.

Summary

Who: Biodiversity, the variety of life on Earth
What: Is imperiled
Where: Worldwide
When: Currently
Why: Loss of species can have a long-lasting, devastating effect
How: Three major threats: habitat destruction, introduction of non-native species, and overexploitation

Sample:

Biodiversity, the variety of life on Earth, is currently imperiled. Since the loss of species can have long-lasting, devastating effects, scientists are concerned about three major threats: habitat destruction, the introduction of species, and overexploitation.

Each step leads to the next in understanding and subject mastery. Basically, I tell my students at the beginning of the year that biology is like a foreign language. Many of the terms are Greek or Latin. They need to be able to break apart words and learn from the prefix, root term, and suffix in order to understand the terms. I also tell them that learning each concept will be the building blocks for the future. For example, whales are mammals, but they are made of eukaryote cells. *Eukaryote* means "true nucleus" and is a type of cell with certain properties. Mammals are members of the Class Mammalia of the Kingdom Animalia. They are also members of the subphylum Vertebrata, meaning that they have a backbone. Mammals are classified as having dentition, mammary glands (modified sweat glands for feeding the young), and hair or fur. Some species of whales have vestigial pelvic girdles, because they once had feet when they lived on land. Long, long ago they returned to a marine habitat because it offered a better ecological niche. As you can see, vocabulary is critical in biology!

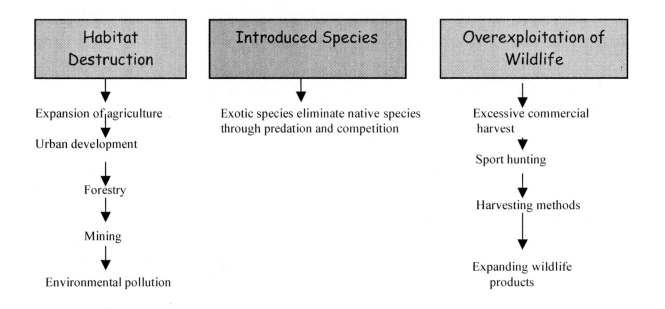

Quiz: The Biodiversity Crisis

True/False

___1. Scientists are very concerned about the biodiversity crisis because they have recently calculated and know the full scale of the loss of species.

___2. In the past 40 years, population densities of migratory songbirds in the mid-Atlantic states have dropped by 50 percent.

___3. One of the main causes of the biodiversity crisis is species inter-mating.

Multiple Choice

___4. Modern mass extinction is different from earlier biodiversity in what way?

    a. "Disaster Species" were predators of "Gentle" animals that serve as food.
    b. "Good" animals were spared.
    c. Prehistoric crashes were all followed by rebounds in diversity.
    d. Gentle animals evolved into disaster species.

___5. Members of the Hundred Heartbeat Club

    a. are species with fewer than 100 individuals left on Earth.
    b. are species whose hearts beat 100 times or more a minute.
    c. are species that were historically destroyed but were necessary to promoting healthy human hearts.
    d. are species that caused the destruction of healthy human hearts.

Chapter 22: Physical Sciences/Mathematics
Selection 34. Are Lotteries Fair?

Reading Level: 14

Introduction

- Begin by asking your students if they feel the lottery is a good idea or bad idea. Actually count the show of hands and write the numbers on the board. Ask how many play the lottery and how often. Never? A few times a year? Every month? Every week? Has anyone ever won? How much did they win compared to how much they have spent over the years of playing?
- Ask if they know where the proceeds go. Have they ever seen a direct result from lottery revenues?
- Share with them the opinion of most mathematicians about gambling on the Internet. It is their view that Internet gambling is programmed to win no matter how good you are, if you are playing for real money. If you are playing for fun, on the other hand, you will win significantly more. Why would this be true? To tempt you to play?
- Talk about luck and students' experiences with luck. How much has luck really helped them?

Follow-Up

- Ask students if this selection changed their minds about playing the lottery. Count hands again and compare to previous results. Question those who changed their minds and ask what persuaded them to think differently. Ask students to identify exactly what the authors used to try to convince the reader to accept their viewpoint.
- Direct the students' attention to the tables and use of statistics in this article. Ask them to predict the kinds of questions that might appear on a test. Do they think they would need to memorize the exact numbers, or would they need to be able to make generalizations instead? Point out that the most important concepts of this article are the generalizations. The statistics are used for validity.
- Remind students that there are both sides to an argument. Ask students to fill out the visual chart on the following page.

Are Lotteries Fair?

PROS	CONS

Conclusion: _____

Quiz: Are Lotteries Fair?

True/False

___ 1. According to this selection, most Americans approve of the lottery and legal gambling in general.

___ 2. One study concluded that money spent from lottery revenues benefits all income levels equally.

___ 3. The conclusion can be made that the higher a person's level of education, the more money the person is likely to spend on the lottery.

Multiple Choice

___ 4. One positive aspect of the lottery is

    a. the reluctance of people with high levels of education to buy tickets.
    b. the increased number of locations in lower income areas for people to buy lottery tickets.
    c. the revenue generated by the lottery that is used for education, recreation, and government initiatives.
    d. the significant improvement to low-income areas as a result of the proceeds from lottery revenues.

___ 5. According to the information in this article, lottery proceeds would mostly likely be used to

    a. construct new playing fields for a city's recreational use.
    b. build a new racetrack to attract tourists.
    c. build a homeless shelter in the city's low income area.
    d. remodel and refurbish government-subsidized housing in a run-down area.

Reading Level: 15

Introduction

- Write the quote on the board, "To go boldly where no one has gone before," and ask students if they recognize this lead-in to a popular television series—*Star Trek*. Spend a few moments discussing space exploration and the dream of the secrets it may reveal for the future of mankind.

- Ask students to recall movies they have seen about outer space. Specifically point out those that have centered around life in outer space—*Star Wars*, *E.T.*, and *Close Encounters of the Third Kind* are movies from their parents' generation. What are some of the more recent movies? How do they differ? How reasonable an idea is the possibility of life on other plants?

- Ask students to think about what would be necessary for life on other planets. Write their ideas on the board.

Follow-Up

- Ask students to read the passage silently and see if any of their own ideas were mentioned in the passage.

- Point out the signals in the selection that reveal the importance of textual information—the subheadings in bold-faced print, the indented list of items that is numbered, the words in bold-faced print. Remind students that these are just like flags signaling important information. Ask students what changes they would make to the subheadings when taking notes on this article. While the subheadings point to important concepts, how could they be turned into questions to be more useful for study purposes?

  Why Life Seems Likely = What reasons are listed that suggest that life might exist elsewhere?
  Prospects for Finding Life in Our Solar System = What are the prospects...?
  The Impact of Finding Life on Human Perspective = How would finding life on other planets impact our own perspective?
  Significance of the Search Itself = What are the benefits of the search for life?

- Instruct students to work in pairs and complete the mapping exercise on page 557 of their textbook for Part D: Reviewing and Organizing Ideas.

- Remind students that science also involves the names of past scientists and their discoveries. Ask them to complete the chart on the next page. Can they think of any others who should be included who are not mentioned in the article?

Notable Figures in Space Exploration

Scientist	Discovery
Copernicus	
Galileo	
Kepler	
Newton	
(other)	

Quiz: Is There Life Elsewhere?

True/False

___1. Scientists have proven the existence of life on other planets in outer space.

___2. It is entirely possible that life on other planets could be completely different, genetically speaking, from our own.

___3. Scientists agree that the discovery of intelligent life on other planets would most likely be very threatening to the existence of life on Earth.

Multiple Choice

___4. Many scientist believe that, if we were to discover only a very simple form of microbial life on another planet instead of extraterrestrial intelligence, this discovery

      a. would have very little impact for us.
      b. would still have profound significance for us.
      c. would indicate that the origin of life is unique to earth.
      d. would prove that intelligent life does not exist elsewhere.

___5. All of the following are mentioned as benefits in the search for alien life *except*

      a. Studying it will help us understand what characteristics of terrestrial life are unique to Earth and what characteristics apply generally to life anywhere.
      b. We would learn much more about the nature of intelligence and might be exposed to cultures and societies very different from those of humans.
      c. We could learn how to arm ourselves against alien threats, discover other worlds to inhabit should ours become unlivable, and assert control over space technology to keep it out of the hands of corrupt individuals or destructive countries.
      d. We could learn the secrets of the nature of the universe, the nature of consciousness and the mind, and the technological marvels that could dramatically change our life here on Earth.

Reading Level: 17

Introduction

- Ask one student to pick a number between one and ten. Using the student's answer, write the phrase "global warming" on the board and ask the students to name (X) amount of facts which they can associate with global warming. This will usually generate a few chuckles and gets the students warmed up to the subject. Accept all answers and praise them for their contributions.
- Remind students of the strategies they should use when reading about physical science and mathematics: Read slowly and reread, if necessary; focus on new terminology; and use writing to learn.
- After students have previewed this article, read the first paragraph out loud. Point out that the density of ideas in this selection is much greater than in many of the others. This article is very technical in nature and students will probably have to reread parts of it several times to understand its meaning.

Follow-Up

- After students have read the selection, remind them to reread any parts they did not understand, and then highlight and annotate important information.
- Ask them to close their books and then circle the room round-robin asking them to recall any details which they can remember. Once they have exhausted all answers, ask students to look at the information and find the ideas that relate to one another. Use colored chalk to put an A beside items in one category, a B beside items in another, and so on.
- Put students into groups and assign them a category to organize into a visual aide for study purposes. Give them a blank overhead transparency and a marking pen to write their final version. Instruct them to open their books and scour the selection to see if any important information in that category should be added. (Place a transparency of the important terms on the next page for students to use after they have worked for awhile on their own.) Continue to remind students to put ideas in their own words and to simplify.
- As a final activity, ask students to explain in their own words the effects of air pollution on global warming and the earth's temperature and weather.

Summary
Sample:

Human activities are responsible for increasing rate of global warming. Consequently, this could change weather patterns, resulting in a severe impact on growing seasons.

Important Terminology

Infrared
Wavelengths
Nanometers
Greenhouse effect
Atmospheric carbon dioxide levels
Industrial Revolution
Atmospheric pollutants
Sulfur dioxide
Global atmospheric resevoir of carbon dioxide
Fossil-fuel emissions
Alkaline
Photosynthesis
Combustion
Deforestation
Evaporate
Reflecting sunlight
Precipitating rain
Rainforests
Arid land
Energy-efficient technologies
Global warming
Variables
Aerosols
Ice sheets
Solar radiation
Glaciers
Thermal expansion
Climatologists
El Niño
Fertile land
Barren land

Quiz: Air Pollution May Result
in Global Warming

True/False

____1. The greenhouse effect helps to keep the earth warm.

____2. Increased carbon-dioxide levels may result in global warming.

____3. Small changes in average global temperatures would probably have very little effect on the world's climate.

Multiple Choice

____4. The majority of global carbon-dioxide emissions are coming primarily from

        a. clearing land for farming.
        b. the burning of fossil fuels.
        c. aerosol sprays.
        d. the oceans, lakes, and rivers.

____5. Deforestation of tropical rainforests presents the problem of

        a. burning wood that releases carbon dioxide into the atmosphere.
        b. destroying a net absorber of carbon dioxide.
        c. decreasing the Earth's capacity to evaporate vast volumes of water vapor, which assist in the formation of clouds.
        d. All of the above.

Reading Level: 10

Introduction

- With the students, brainstorm achievements of which they are proud. Then ask them to analyze the personal skills that were needed to accomplish each of those achievements. Which ones might be useful to a future employer?
- Ask students how many times they have seen their parents change jobs.
- Ask the students about the following statement: "Additional training, not money, is most valued by employees because it makes them feel valued." Do they agree with this statement?

Follow-Up

- Ask the students to divide an index card into two columns. On one side, they are to indicate adjectives that describe themselves. On the other side, they are to indicate adjectives that describe the job for which they are preparing. Divide the students into groups and have them create lists of ten words, using new vocabulary words when appropriate. Then bring students back into a group and create a master list. Explain that speculating about what kinds of words may appear on the list could help them prepare for interview situations.

Summary

Who: Analysis of personal qualities
What: Preparing for a career
When: While in college
Where: Anywhere
Why: Knowing your abilities and qualifications
How: Interest inventories, personality tests, self-analyses

Sample:

Through interest inventories, personality tests, and self-analyses, students should assess their personal qualities, abilities, and qualifications while in college to help them find the best career path.

Quiz: Building Toward a Career

True/False

___1. Aptitude tests and personality tests are invaluable aids for job hunting because they will reveal the perfect job for the taker.

___2. An employment portfolio consists of information and research that students collect about companies they are considering for employment.

___3. Analyzing personal interests, characteristics, and capabilities will help students identify occupations and companies where they might be happy working.

Multiple Choice

___4. All of the following are mentioned in discovering what might bring students satisfaction *except*

        a. compensation.
        b. size of the company.
        c. corporate clients.
        d. corporate culture.

___5. The author suggests that students can build toward their career by

        a. taking temporary assignments.
        b. keeping a journal about their interview experiences.
        c. updating their skills.
        d. both A and C.

Reading Level: 9

Introduction

- Write the following quotation on the board:

  "The greatest cure of anger is delay."   Seneca

  Ask students their opinion of the quotation. Since the quotation appears in the selection, have them predict some strategies that will be introduced. Also, ask if they have some personal, positive strategies they have developed for dealing with anger.   Do they succumb to the temptation of road rage? Some psychologists believe that those who feel they have no control over their lives cannot control their anger. Do the students agree or disagree with this?
- Ask the students to share their thoughts on the following: The major cause of low morale in the workplace is a lack of leadership.

Follow-Up

- Before students complete the outline in the text, have them brainstorm what they can recall and help them organize the material with the conceptual map on the next page.

Summary

Who:	Experts
What:	Offer strategies to deal with anger
Where:	In the workplace
When:	At any time
Why:	To make the job more enjoyable and the position more secure
How:	Using humor and changing your perspective

Sample:

In order to make a job more enjoyable and a position more secure, employees can deal more effectively with anger in the workplace by considering some expert strategies using humor and changing their perspective.

What Makes Us Angry	Causes of Illegitimate Anger	How to Avoid Feeling Out of Control

Dealing with an incompetent boss
▼
Being maligned by co-workers
▼
Failing to get a deserved promotion
▼
The critical boss
▼
Being left out by peers

Selfishness
↓
Perfectionism
↓
Paranoia

Accept anger
↓
Acknowledge choices
↓
Cool anger with humor
↓
Practice forgiveness

Quiz: Rx for Anger at Work

True/False

____1. According to Dr. Hendrie Weisinger, there are three major work situations that can provoke anger.

____2. The best reason to learn to deal with anger is to avoid stress and keep your job.

____3. Workplace rumors frequently cause irrevocable damage.

Multiple Choice

____4. The main causes of illegitimate behavior in the workplace include all of the following *except*

      a. boredom.
      b. paranoia.
      c. selfishness.
      d. perfectionism.

____5. According to the article, which coping technique was not mentioned for dealing with anger when you feel out of control?

      a. acceptance of the anger.
      b. journal writing.
      c. acknowledging choices.
      d. practicing forgiveness.

Reading Level: 10.5

Introduction

- Remind students of the tips for reading about the workplace: Focus on practical information; pay attention to trends and projections; apply what you learn.
- Poll students on their sleep habits. Since many have jobs and families and school, they may not be getting enough rest. Also, ask how many eat vegetables daily. How many get some kind of daily exercise? How many are able to successfully manage their stress?
- Share with students the recent statistics that indicate that adults who sleep an average of five hours or fewer a night have a 40% lower insulin sensitivity than those who have eight or more hours. Therefore, researchers speculate that they are more likely to develop diabetes and gain weight faster.

Follow-Up

- Brainstorm and organize according to the map in the text on page 599.

Summary

Who:	Sleep-deprived adults
What:	Suffer physically and cognitively
When:	When they get fewer than eight hours of sleep
Where:	Effects are seen in daily life and workplace
Why:	Sleep stages are vital to general physical and mental health
How:	Affects our immune system and neural activity which affects our memory, moods, and energy levels

Sample:

Though a growing trend, sleep-deprived adults experience health and cognitive detriment when they get fewer than eight hours of sleep a night; the effect extends to many careers and can have devastating consequences in all activities, including memory, moods, and energy levels.

Quiz: The Sandman Is Dead   Long Live
the Sleep Deprived Walking Zombie

True/False

____1. One way to prevent the harmful effects of sleep deprivation is to provide opportunities for shift work.

____2. Americans are generally ignorant when it comes to the importance of the facts and myths about sleep.

____3. You need more sleep as you get older.

Multiple Choice

____4. According to the National Sleep Foundation survey, approximately what percentage of American adults tested reached levels of sleepiness known to be dangerous?

      a. 25%
      b. 33%
      c. 50%
      d. 75%

____5. To which practice would the authors advise employers to adhere?

      a. create shift work for employees.
      b. provide nap time as is done in many kindergartens.
      c. require four-day work weeks, so employees can catch up on lost sleep.
      d. offer bonuses to workers who document getting at least eight hours of sleep, since the health benefits often save money.

Reading Level: 13

Introduction

- Explain to students that even when a professor assigns long reading selections—and there will be times when several long chapters are assigned for a following lecture—they should break them into manageable chunks as we will do in our class.
- Have students read silently the scenario of Mr. Peairs' shooting of Yoshihiro Hittori. Ask them if this could happen in their community. Would such an incident occur in other cultures? If you have ESL students or students who have lived in other countries, encourage them to give their opinions based on their personal experiences.
- Ask students for their thoughts on the following quotation by Milgram, "We are all fragile creatures intertwined in a cobweb of social constraints."

Follow-Up

- After previewing and reading, have students practice some of the strategies which they have learned. List some vocabulary words from the section and ask students to create "concept cards" by writing the word on one card with the definition, example, and visual on the back. (For hands-on learners, mention that they should create another set of cards with the definition only, so they can play a memory game and match the words and definitions. Since the correct definition is on the back, the activity will be self-checking for them.)
- Vocabulary Words: *roles, norms, social psychologists, cultural psychologists*
- Have students summarize the Milgram experiment and the prison study.
- Create a conceptual map for the power of roles.

Quiz: Roles and Rules

True/False

____1. The "cobweb of social constraints" consists of social norms.

____2. Positions regulated by norms about how people should behave are called principles.

____3. The Milgram study investigated the way people's aggression overcomes their judgment.

Multiple Choice

____4. According to the selection, the roles which people fill consist of all of the following *except*

        a. gender.
        b. romantic.
        c. occupational.
        d. family.

____5. Critics of the Milgram experiment complained about all of the following *except*

        a. It was invalid because subjects were told in advance about the desired outcome.
        b. It was unethical because subjects suffered emotional pain.
        c. The conclusion that situation overrules personality may not be valid since some personality traits such as hostility and authoritarianism predict obedience.
        d. They objected to the parallel drawn between the subjects and Nazi doctors.

Reading Level: 13

Introduction

- Review terms and experiments from the previous reading.
- Explain that critical reading is crucial in this selection, so students may want to review the process in Part I.

Follow-Up

- Ask the students create concept cards using the following terms from the selection: *social cognition, social identities, ethnic identity, acculturation, attribution theory, situational attribution, dispositional attribution, fundamental attribution error, self-serving bias, just-world hypothesis, cognitive dissonance, validity effect.*
- Have the students complete the guided note-taking activity on the next page of the manual.
- Use the conceptual map on page 186 for an overview of ways to influence people.
- Discuss some mnemonic devices which students can create to learn some words and definitions.

Term	Definition
Social Cognition	An area in social psychology concerned with social influences on thought, memory, perception, and other cognitive processes.
Social Identities	*Aspects of our self-concepts that area based on nationality, ethnicity, religion, and social roles*
Ethnic Identity	A close identification with a religious or ethnic group.
Acculturation	An identification with a dominant culture.
Attribution Theory	The theory that people are motivated to explain their own and other people's behavior by attributing causes of that behavior to a situation or a disposition.
Situational Attribution	Identifying something in the environment as a cause of an action.
Dispositional Attribution	*Identifying a person's traits or motives as the cause of an action.*
Fundamental Attribution Error	The tendency to explain other people's behavior by overestimating personality factors and underestimating the influence of the situation.
Self-serving bias	The tendency to choose attributions that are favorable to one, taking credit for good actions but letting the situation account for the bad one.
Just-world Hypothesis	The notion that many people need to believe that the world is fair and that justice is served, that bad people are punished and good people are rewarded.
Cognitive Dissonance	A state of tension that occurs when a person simultaneously holds two cognitions that are psychologically inconsistent, or when a person's belief is incongruent with his or her behavior.
Validity Effect	The tendency of people to believe that a statement is true or valid simply because it has been repeated many times.

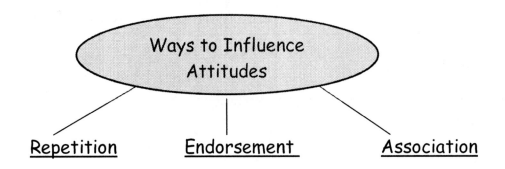

Repetition   Endorsement   Association

Quiz: Identity, Attributions, and Attitudes

True/False

___1. According to Arkes (1991), the repetition of an idea seems to increase the perception of its validity.

___2. Another term for "The Big Lie" is cognitive dissonance.

___3. Americans tend to feel that the major political and social changes that occurred when they were between the ages of 16-24 were most critical in terms of self-definition.

Multiple Choice

___4. A person who has weak feelings of ethnicity but a strong sense of acculturation is described as

        a. bicultural.
        b. marginal.
        c. assimilated.
        d. separatist.

___5. Which process below would not be used in coercive persuasiveness?

        a. A person is put under emotional and physical distress.
        b. A leader offers unconditional love, acceptance, and attention.
        c. Access to information is readily shared.
        d. A new identity based on the group is created.

Chapter 24: Psychology Textbook Chapter
Psychology Selection 3: Individuals in Groups

Reading Level: 12

Introduction

- Begin by reading the last paragraph aloud.
- Discuss the questions presented and ask students if they have ever had the opportunity to meet some of the challenges, such as calling 911.

Follow-Up

- Have students create concept cards for the following terms: *groupthink; diffusion of responsibility; deindividuation; social loafing; altruism.*
- Provide students with a copy of the process diagram on the next page and use it as a guided note-taking activity.
- Ask the students to consider any parallels to altruism,whistle-blowing, groupthink, or diffusion of responsiblity in films they have seen recently such as *Erin Brockovich, Proof of Life, The Art of War*, and *Hurricane.*
- Have the students create a conceptual map of the symptoms of groupthink similar to the one on page 190.

Factors That Predict Independent Actions

1. The individual perceives the need for intervention or help.

   ↓

2. The individual decides to take responsibility

   ↓

3. *The individual decides that the costs of doing nothing outweigh the costs of getting involved.*

   ↓

4. The individual has an ally.

   ↓

5. *The individual becomes entrapped.*

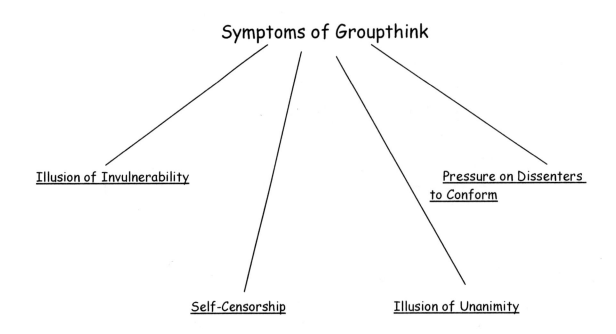

Symptoms of Groupthink

Illusion of Invulnerability

Self-Censorship

Pressure on Dissenters to Conform

Illusion of Unanimity

Quiz: Individuals in Groups

True/False

___1. Generally, the decisions which group members make and the actions they take depend least on the structure and dynamics of the group itself.

___2. The phenomenon of groupthink is so strong that it is impossible to counteract.

___3. Social loafing, when each member slows down and allows others to work harder, is a form of diffusion of responsibility.

Multiple Choice

___4. Which of the items below is not a symptom of groupthink?

        a. Illusion of invulnerability.
        b. Self-censorship.
        c. Direct pressure on dissenters to conform.
        d. Illusion of anonymity.

___5. Some social and situational factors that predict independent actions, such as whistle-blowing, include all of the following *except*

        a. Individual perceives a need for intervention or help.
        b. Individual decides to take responsibility.
        c. Individual is a loner who enjoys instigating chaos.
        d. Costs of doing nothing outweigh the costs of doing something.

Reading Level: 12

Introduction

- Review the terms *connotation* and *denotation*. Also, ask students for examples for euphemisms.
- Begin by playing the song "You've Got to Be Taught" from *South Pacific.*
- Preview the film *I'll Remember April* and show a clip to demonstrate the prejudice imposed on Japanese Americans during World War II.
- Ask students to discuss other examples of prejudice against other cultures. Ask them if the instances are the result of fear or simply a lack of understanding.
- Teach the students the definition of *xenophobia* by pointing out that *xeno* means *stranger* and *phobia* means *fear*.

Follow-Up

- Have students create concept cards to study the following terms: *ethnocentrism; relativist; absolutist; stereotype; prejudice contact hypothesis.*
- Ask the students complete the guided note-taking activity on the next page.
- Have students to complete summary cards on the Robbers' Cave Study.
- Have students create a process diagram on how to end prejudice on page 194.
- Point out the conditions that must exist for the greatest impact of eliminating prejudice on page 195.

Term	Explanation
Ethnocentrism	A person's belief that his or her own ethnic group, nation, or religion is superior to all others.
Relativist Position	The argument that cultures should be judged strictly on their own terms and not judged by the customs of others even when those customs cause suffering and death.
Absolutist Position	The argument that when cultures violate certain universal human rights, the correct response is moral indignation and censure.
Stereotype	*A cognitive schema or a summary impression of a group, in which a person believes that all members of the group share a common trait or traits (positive, negative or neutral).*
Prejudice	A negative stereotype and a strong, unreasonable dislike or hatred of a group or a cultural practice.
Contact Hypothesis	The approach that the best way to end prejudice is to bring members of both sides together and let them get acquainted; in the this way, they will discover their shared humanity.

How to End Prejudice by Changing People's Circumstances

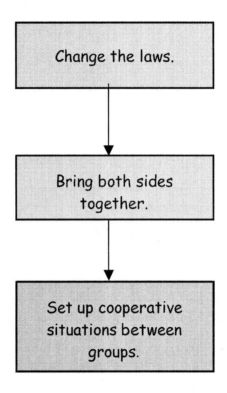

Change the laws.

Bring both sides together.

Set up cooperative situations between groups.

Four Conditions Required to Make the Greatest Impact on Eliminating Prejudice

Both must have
equal status
and equal economic
standing.

Both must cooperate
working together for
a common goal.

Both must have
moral, legal, and
economic support
of authorities.

Both must have
opportunities to work
and socialize
together.

Quiz: Cross-Cultural Relations

True/False

___1. The most important reason for prejudice, in the sociocultural view, is that it brings economic benefits to the majority group and justifies its dominance.

___2. All prejudices have deep-seated psychological roots.

___3. The belief that your own culture is superior to all others is called ethnocentrism.

Multiple Choice

___4. Stereotypes distort reality in all but which of the following ways?

    a. Exaggerate differences between groups.
    b. Produce selective perception.
    c. Underestimate differences within other groups.
    d. Underestimate similarities between groups.

___5. The process to end prejudice includes all of the following *except*

    a. allowing people's circumstances to remain unchanged.
    b. allowing both sides to have contact and get acquainted.
    c. setting up cooperative situations among antagonistic groups.
    d. changing people's circumstances.

Psychology Jeopardy

Roles and Rules	Identity, Attribution, and Attitudes	Individuals in Groups	Cross-Cultural Relations
Define *norms.*	Explain the role of researchers of social cognition.	Explain the experiment of Soloman Asch.	Define *ethnocentrism.*
Define *role.*	Social identities, aspects of ourselves, are based on what four roles?	Define *groupthink.*	Explain three ways that stereotypes can distort reality.
Explain the Milgram experiment.	Define *acculturation.*	List four conditions that can result in groupthink.	Give an example of a positive and a negative stereotype.
List three criticisms of the Milgram experiment.	Explain the two categories of attribution theory.	Define *diffusion of responsibility* and give a famous case as an example.	Define symbolic racism.
Explain the prison study.	Explain *cognitive dissonance.*	Define *social loafing.*	Explain the link between economic conditions and scapegoating in America.
List four factors that cause people to obey when they would rather not.	What is another name for "The Big Lie"?	When members of a group lose all awareness of their individuality and sense of self, the state is called _____.	Explain *contact hypothesis.*
Summarize Milgram's Experiment.	List three ways to effectively influence attitudes.	List five social and situational factors that predict independent actions such as whistle-blowing.	What four conditions must be met in order to have an impact in eliminating prejudice?

Reading Level: 17

Introduction

- Ask the students to reveal what they ate the day before. Ask them to analyze the nutritional value of the food they consumed.
- What kinds of problems arise from poor nutrition? What do they know about eating disorders?

- Invite the students to explore the government nutritional site on the Internet (http://www.mypyramid.org). Students can find an assessment of their diet quality, find dietary guidelines, track their physical activity, and read the truth about healthy eating. Ask students to keep track of their diets by writing down everything they eat in a daily journal. Explain that they will keep this log until the end of the unit.

Follow-Up

- After the students have previewed and read the passage, ask them to recall details with closed texts as you write the details on the board. After they have all had a chance to offer a detail, ask them to open their text and verify their answers.

- Next, to provide an overview of what they can recall, have the students complete the conceptual map on the following page. (Block out the answers.)

- Provide students with the guided note-taking activity on page 199 to organize the ideas in this section.

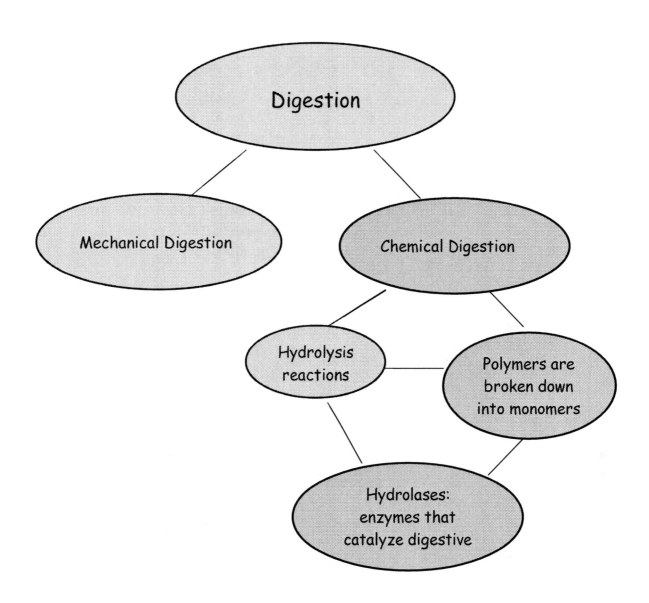

STAGES OF FOOD PROCESSING

Stage	Process
Ingestion:	eating
Digestion:	breakdown of food into small molecules such as simple sugars and amino acids mechanical digestion = chewing chemical digestion = chemical breakdown of food by digestive enzymes
Absorption:	the uptake of small nutrient molecules by cells lining the digestive tract
Elimination:	the disposal of leftover undigested materials

Quiz: Overview of Animal Nutrition

True/False

____1. The uptake of the small nutrient molecules by cells lining the digestive tract is known as digestion.

____2. During and after chewing, food is exposed to digestive enzymes that break down the large food molecules into monomers.

____3. Most of the molecules of food (polymers) are exactly like the polymers that make up an animal's body.

Multiple Choice

____4. Animals can digest food without digesting their own cells and tissues because

        a. the digestive enzymes will not break down regular cells.
        b. the specific digestive enzymes react only to food.
        c. there are no digestive enzymes in the stomachs of animals, because these exist only in the mouth.
        d. the chemical digestion of food proceeds safely within some kind of compartment.

____5. Animals that gain nutrients from both plants and animals are known as

        a. omnivores.
        b. herbivores.
        c. carnivores.
        d. vegans.

Reading Level: 11

Introduction

- Discuss the changes which students have noticed in the makeup of their diets over the past years. What about their friends? Other ethnic groups? How are their views toward eating different from their grandparents' attitudes?
- If possible, take students to the following online site: http://www.innerbody.com/htm/body.html. This is a human anatomy site that allows students to visually trace the digestive system throughout the body and see the parts as they appear in the body. Explain that they will be reading about the digestive system, and they will find it helpful if they can visualize the process as they read.
- Finally, remind students about the necessity of learning specialized terms while studying biology. Ask them to highlight all of the terminology specific to the digestive system.

Follow-Up

- With the class, create the conceptual map on the following page. Divide the class into groups of two or three and ask them to list the major components of the digestive system. What additional information can they remember?
- Provide the guided note-taking activity on page 203 of the manual to organize the information on the digestive system from this text chapter. Divide the information among groups of students and ask them to explain their portion to the class. Then ask students to complete the chart from memory on page 719 of their textbook
- Invite a biology instructor to the class to discuss the information the students have learned about digestion. What information would he or she expect students to know in order to handle a test successfully?
- Bring in inexpensive playdough and ask the students to re-create the human digestive system in small groups. Give "prizes" for the most realistic representations. "Smarties" go to the first prize winners.
- Summarize the significance of Figure 22.11, "Ulcer-causing bacteria."

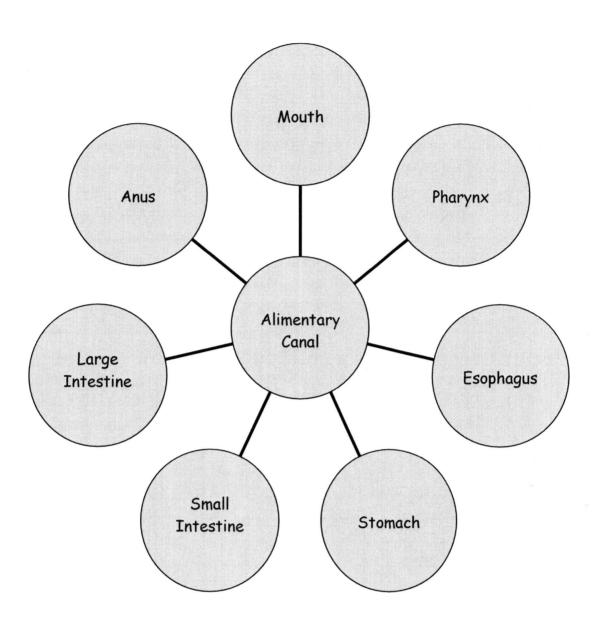

Digestive System	Definition and Function
Alimentary canal	
Salivary amylase	
Pharynx	
Trachea	
Windpipe	
Epiglottis	
Esophagus	
Peristalsis	
Stomach	
Gastric juice	
Acid chime	
Pepsin	
Sphincters	
Small intestine	
Duodenum	
Bile	
Gallbladder	
Hydrolase	
Epithelium	
Large intestine	
Colon	
Feces	

Quiz: A Tour of the Human Digestive System

True/False

___1. The alimentary canal is distinctive in humans because it has only one opening to allow for the processing of food.

___2. The small intestine is appropriately named because it is the smallest part of the alimentary canal.

___3. Nutrients are considered "in" the body once they have entered the alimentary canal and been broken down into food molecules.

Multiple Choice

___4. With which statement below would the authors disagree?

    a. The stomach wall can stretch to accommodate enough food to sustain us for several hours.
    b. The stomach will not eat itself because of a protective coating of mucus and because the secretion of gastric juice is regulated so that it is discharged only when food is in the stomach.
    c. It takes about 24 hours for the stomach to empty after a meal.
    d. The cause of most ulcers is not stress.

___5. The major organ for chemical digestion and for absorption of nutrients into the bloodstream is the

    a. esophagus.
    b. stomach.
    c. small intestine.
    d. large intestine.

Chapter 25: Biology Textbook Chapter
Biology Selection 3. Human Nutritional Requirements and Nutritional Disorders

Reading Level: 14

Introduction

- Ask the students to analyze their food journals. What trends do they see in their eating? How does their diet compare with the information about nutrition they learned from their search for information on the Internet?
- What memories do students associate with food? Can they pinpoint the influences that affect the healthy or unhealthy ways they are eating? Why is our society becoming more obese?
- Survey the class to determine if the students know of any people with eating disorders. What do they already know about eating disorders?

Follow-Up

- Use the guided note-taking activity for nutritional issues found on the next page of this manual.
- Ask students to complete the outline that begins on page 727 of their text to organize the information on human nutritional requirements.
- Use the Nutrition and Digestion Jeopardy game on page 208 of the manual for a review of the biology chapter.

Nutrition Information

Food as Fuel	• Calories • Metabolic rate • The official food-guide pyramid • Caloric balance
Food as Building Material	• Essential nutrients. • Essential amino acids. • Vitamins
Decoding Food Labels	• Ingredients • Nutritional information
Nutritional Disorders	• Malnutrition • Obesity • Fat cravings

Biology Jeopardy

Animal Nutrition	Human Digestive System	Nutritional Requirements and Nutritional Disorders
Most chemical digestion occurs in the _____.	Define alimentary canal.	Metabolic rate can be defined as _____.
The four stages of food processing are _____.	Peristalsis is the _____.	Explain how people gain weight.
The main difference between digestive sacs and digestive tubes is _____.	The trachea is protected from food by the _____.	Energy stored in food is measured by _____.
Food polymers are broken down into _____.	The stomach lining is replaced about _____.	Describe the components of a healthy diet.
Mechanical digestion is the process of _____.	Heartburn is actually caused by _____.	What are the two types or information found on food labels?
Elimination is the _____.	The longest part of the alimentary canal is the _____.	Define malnutrition.
Herbivores eat mainly _____.	Describe how nutrients are absorbed into the body.	Explain why we are predisposed to crave fat.

Quiz: Human Nutritional Requirements and Nutritional Disorders

True/False

___1. The rate of energy consumption by the body is called cellular respiration.

___2. Essential amino acids cannot be made in our bodies and must be obtained from eating specific foods.

___3. Humans have been programmed from an evolutionary standpoint to eat fatty foods.

Multiple Choice

___4. The energy stored in food and expended during daily activities can be measured in

       a. calories.
       b. metabolic rate.
       c. cellular respiration.
       d. essential amino acids.

___5. If you take in more by eating than you burn by activity, you will

       a. lose weight.
       b. gain weight.
       c. develop a food disorder.
       d. become malnourished.

Options to Instructional Strategies for Psychology and Biology Text Readings

Option One

- Divide the class into groups and assign a reading section from one of the chapters to each group. Within the groups, assign jobs to students by adapting the suggestions of Harvey Daniels in *Literature Circles: Voice and Choice in the Student-Centered Classroom* (Stenhouse Publishers, York, ME, 1994).

- Within the group, designate a *leader, note-taker, quotation-gatherer* (someone who locates significant quotations from the readings that might appear on tests or might be useful in essays), *summarizer* (someone who organizes details and leads the group in summary writing related to the reading), *reader, questioner* (someone who directs the group to contrive test questions and creates a short quiz to give classmates), and *artist* (someone who creates a visual such as a concept map or process diagram). When the group members have completed their assignment on the section, they are to make a presentation and teach the selection. As a Follow-Up, they can quiz the students as they would in a study group to determine how prepared the students are.

Option Two

- Collaborate with colleagues who teach psychology and biology. Videotape a class lecture based on one of the chapter selections, then have the students compare notes taken during their reading to those taken during the lecture they view. Finally, create study groups to prepare for an actual test prepared by the psychology or history instructors.

Option Three

- Use a jigsaw learning activity as a collaborative peer-teaching opportunity. With this option, every student is given a chance to teach something. First, the four readings in the psychology chapter could initially be divided up and later presented as a whole. Likewise, the three sections in the history chapter could be similarly segmented and then later presented as one chapter.

- To create a jigsaw situation, for example, assign each psychology reading to a different group so that you initially have four groups. Next, ask the students to follow guidelines such as 1: summarize sections within their paragraph; 2: create a visual; 3: organize a guided note-taking activity; 4: create a game for learning a concept; 5: search the Internet for additional information. After each group has its work, members move to a different group, so each person in the new group will teach what he knows about his or her reading.

Part IV: Useful Teaching Materials

Three-Minute Paper

- What Is One Thing You Learned Today?

- What Else Do You Feel You Need to Learn?

- What Is One Question You Wish You Had Asked Before the End of the Class?

Send Me An E-mail

- Tell me how it's going so far.
- What do you think is your strength in the class?
- What do you hope to improve most in the class?

Reading levels on Part II selections are listed below in order of appearance and are based on Fry Graph calculations.

Part II Reading Selections	Fry Graph Reading Level
1. Urban Legends	7
2. The New Flirting Game	10
3. Coming into My Own	7
4. Reality TV: Race to the Bottom	12
5. War: The Mother of All Words	11
6. Lovers	11
7. To Love and to Cherish	11
8. Peti's Malu: Traditions of Samoan Tattooing	7
9. Play, Leisure, and Culture	13
10. Should Students Attend School Year Round? Yes	13.5
11. Should Students Attend School Year Round? No	10
12. His Name Is Michael	8
13. Shaping Her People's Heritage: Nampeyo (1852-1942)	12
14. Gregory	5
15. The Truth Is	4
16. The Effects of the Minimum Wage	9
17. When Living Is a Fate Worse Than Death	7.5
18. Seoul Searching	5
19. The Beautiful Laughing Sisters—An Arrival Story	9
20. Profile of a Terrorist	16
21. Whether to Vote: A Citizen's First Choice	11
22. Four Simple Words That Guarantee the Job of Your Dreams	7
23. McDonald's Makes a Lot of People Angry for a Lot of Different Reasons	13
24. Hispanic Americans: A Growing Market Segment	12
25. Blogger Beware	14
26. Hold it Right There, and Drop That Camera	10
27. House Arrest and Electronic Monitoring	11
28. Use It and Lose It	9
29. Make No Mistake: Medical Errors Can Be Deadly Serious	15
30. Athletes Looking Good and Doing Better with Anabolic Steroids?	16
31. Honor Among Beasts	11
32. Bugs in Your Pillow	13
33. The Biodiversity Crisis	16
34. Are Lotteries Fair?	14
35. Is There Life Elsewhere?	15
36. Air Pollution May Result in Global Warming	17
37. Building Toward a Career	10
38. Rx for Anger at Work	9
39. The Sandman Is Dead Long Live the Sleep Deprived Walking Zombie	10.5

(Part II reading levels on the selections below. listed in order of difficulty, are based on Fry Graph calculations.)

Part II Reading Selections	Fry Graph Reading Level
1. The Truth Is	4
2. Gregory	5
3. Seoul Searching	5
4. Urban Legends	7
5. Coming into My Own	7
6. Four Simple Words That Guarantee the Job of Your Dreams	7
7. Peti's Malu: Traditions of Samoan Tattooing	7
8. When Living Is a Fate Worse Than Death	7.5
9. His Name Is Michael	8
10. The Effects of the Minimum Wage	9
11. The Beautiful Laughing Sisters—An Arrival Story	9
12. Use It and Lose It	9
13. Rx for Anger at Work	9
14. The New Flirting Game	10
15. Should Students Attend School Year Round? No	10
16. Just Walk on By	10
17. Hold It Right There, and Drop That Camera	10
18. The Sandman Is Dead—Long Live the Sleep-QADeprived Walking Zombie	10.5
19. Lovers	11
20. To Love and to Cherish	11
21. War: The Mother of All Words	11
22. Whether to Vote: A Citizen's First Choice	11
23. Honor Among Beasts	11
24. House Arrest and Electronic Monitoring	11
25. Reality TV: Race to the Bottom	12
26. Shaping People's Heritage: Nampeyo (1852-1942)	12
27. Hispanic Americans: A Growing Market Segment	12
28. Play, Leisure, and Culture	13
29. McDonald's Makes a Lot of People Angry for a Lot of Different Reasons	13
30. Bugs in Your Pillow	13
31. Should Students Attend School Year Round? Yes	13.5
32. Blogger Beware	14
33. Are Lotteries Fair?	14
34. Is There Life Elsewhere?	15
35. Make No Mistake: Medical Errors Can Be Deadly Serious	15
36. Profile of a Terrorist	16
37. Athletes Looking Good and Doing Better with Anabolic Steroids?	16
38. The Biodiversity Crisis	16
39. Air Pollution May Result in Global Warming	17

Sample Syllabus

Instructor:
Office:
Hours:
Voice Mail:
E-mail

We live in a visual culture, one which daily bombards us with images—written and electronic—that we must comprehend, analyze, and synthesize. That is even truer of the experiences of college students who comprehend and evaluate large amounts of material quickly. To do this successfully, the student needs skills in note-taking, time management, vocabulary enhancement, comprehension, critical reading, concise writing, and effective searching of the Web. This course is designed for students who want to raise their academic abilities to the college level and become the competition.

This course is intended to make you more comfortable with words—reading and writing them. Through the study of context clues, word analysis, etymology, connotation and denotation, you will enhance your vocabulary. Through the study of main idea, supporting details, transition words, and writing patterns, you will improve your ability to understand and remember what you have read, and you will demystify the writing process. Through the study of critical reading, which includes making inferences, discerning fact and opinion, recognizing tone, and evaluating written material, you will learn to analyze and evaluate material. In addition, you will practice successful study-skill strategies to make more efficient use of your time and improve your ability to focus. Finally, you will have the opportunity to practice skills learned during the lectures, as well as opportunities to apply those skills while exploring the Internet and learning evaluating technology.

"Books had the power to alter my view of the world forever."—Pat Conroy

Required Materials
McWhorter, K, *Reading Across the Disciplines*
Longman, 2002

College-level dictionary
3x5 index cards
Highlighter and #2 pencils

215

Week 1	Course Introduction
	Active Reading and Thinking Strategies (Chapter 1)
	Attributes of an Active Learner (Chapter 1)
	Previewing (Chapter 1)
	Strategies for Reading Across the Disciplines

Week 2	Strategies for Successful Studying and Organizing Ideas (Chapter 7)
	Vocabulary Building: Context Clues (Chapter 2)
	Readings (How to Study for Social Sciences):
	• Urban Legends
	• The New Flirting Game
	• Coming into My Own

Week 3	Vocabulary Building: Prefixes, Roots, Suffixes (Chapter 2)
	Readings (How to Study for Communication/Speech):
	• Reality TV: Race to the Bottom
	• War: The Mother of All Words
	• Lovers

Week 4	Thesis, Main Idea, Supporting Details, and Transitions (Chapter 3)
	Readings (How to Study for Anthropology):
	• To Love and to Cherish
	• Peti's Malu: Traditions of Samoan Tattooing
	• Play, Leisure, and Culture

Week 5	Thesis, Main Idea, Supporting Details, and Transitions (Chapter 3)
	Readings (How to Study for Education):
	• Should Students Attend School Year Round? Yes
	• Should Students Attend School Year Round? No
	• His Name Is Michael

Week 6	Organizational Patterns (Chapter 4)
	Readings (How to Study for Arts/Humanities/Literature):
	• Shaping Her People's Heritage: Nampeo (1852-1942)
	• Gregory
	• The Truth Is

Week 7	Organizational Patterns (Chapter 4)
	Readings (How to Study for Public Policy/Contemporary Issues):
	• The Effects of the Minimum Wage
	• When Living Is a Fate Worse Than Death
	• Seoul Searching

Week 8	Making Inferences (Chapter 5)
	Readings (How to Study for Political Science/Government/History):
	• The Beautiful Laughing Sisters—An Arrival Story
	• Profile of a Terrorist
	• Whether to Vote: A Citizen's First Choice

Week 9	Critical Reading (Chapter 6)
	Readings (How to Study for Business/Advertising/Economics):
	• Four Simple Words That Guarantee the Job of Your Dreams
	• McDonald's Makes a Lot of People Angry for a Lot of Different Reasons
	• Hispanic Americans: A Growing Market Segment

Week 10	Critical Reading (Chapter 6)
	Readings (How to Study for Technology/Computers):
	• Blogger Beware
	• Hold it Right There, and Drop That Camera
	• House Arrest and Electronic Monitoring

Week 11	Critical Reading (Chapter 7)
	Readings (How to Study for the Health-Related Fields):
	• Use It and Lose It
	• Make No Mistake: Medical Errors Can Be Deadly Serious
	• Athletes Looking Good and Doing Better with Anabolic Steroids?

Week 12	Improving and Adjusting Your Reading Rate (Chapter 8)
	Readings (Studying for Workplace/Career Fields):
	• Building Toward a Career
	• Rx for Anger at Work
	• The Sandman Is Dead—Long Live the Sleep Deprived Walking Zombie

Week 13	Reading and Evaluating Electronic Sources (Chapter 9)
	Readings (Studying for Life Sciences):
	• Honor Among Beasts
	• Bugs in Your Pillow
	• The Biodiversity Crisis

Week 14	Review Strategies for Organizing Ideas (Chapter 7)
	Readings (Studying for Physical Sciences/Mathematics):
	• Are Lotteries Fair?
	• Is There Life Elsewhere
	• Air Pollution May Result in Global Warming

Week 15   Review Strategies for Organizing Ideas (Chapter 7)
               Readings (Studying a Textbook Chapter)
- Psychology Textbook Chapter
- Biology Textbook Chapter

Important Dates:

Classes Begin:
Last Day to Add a Class:
Last Day to Drop for Refund
Last Day to Drop with a Grade of *W*

Classes End:

Final Exam:

"A good reader is one who has imagination, memory, a dictionary, and some artistic sense."—Vladimir Nabokov

Reading Survey
(Pre-Course Personal Assessment)

Choose the letter of the answer that best indicates your feelings and concerns about taking this course.

1. I feel my high school experience adequately prepared me for the academic challenges of college.
  a. strongly agree b. agree c. disagree d. strongly disagree

2. Taking this course is not necessary to my success as a college student.
  a. strongly agree b. agree c. disagree d. strongly disagree

3. My vocabulary is strong and exemplary for an entering college freshman.
  a. strongly agree b. agree c. disagree d. strongly disagree

4. I am comfortable "attacking" new and unfamiliar words and can pronounce them and discern their meaning with ease.
  a. strongly agree b. agree c. disagree d. strongly disagree

5. Although I am comfortable *saying the words* when I read, I cannot always *understand* the content of what I have read.
  a. strongly agree b. agree c. disagree d. strongly disagree

6. Although I am comfortable *saying the words* and comprehending what I have read, I have difficulty *remembering* the content, even right after finishing an assignment.
  a. strongly agree b. agree c. disagree d. strongly disagree

7. Although my reading is adequate, my writing ability needs improvement.
  a. strongly agree b. agree c. disagree d. strongly disagree

8. When I think about taking a math class, I feel uncomfortable.
  a. strongly agree b. agree c. disagree d. strongly disagree

9. I am able to manage my time.
  a. strongly agree b. agree c. disagree d. strongly disagree

10. I have good organizational skills in my academic life.
  a. strongly agree b. agree c. disagree d. strongly disagree

11. I am organized in my personal life.
  a. strongly agree b. agree c. disagree d. strongly disagree

12. I do not procrastinate.
  a. strongly agree b. agree c. disagree d. strongly disagree

13. My reading rate is adequate for my needs.
    a. strongly agree   b. agree   c. disagree   d. strongly disagree

14. Improving my reading rate is a priority for me.
    a. strongly agree   b. agree   c. disagree   d. strongly disagree

15. Improving my vocabulary is a priority for me.
    a. strongly agree   b. agree   c. disagree   d. strongly disagree

16. Improving my comprehension is a priority for me.
    a. strongly agree   b. agree   c. disagree   d. strongly disagree

17. Improving my writing ability is a priority for me.
    a. strongly agree   b. agree   c. disagree   d. strongly disagree

18. I feel that attending and participating in class are essential to academic success.
    a. strongly agree   b. agree   c. disagree   d. strongly disagree

19. I feel that successful students are prepared for class.
    a. strongly agree   b. agree   c. disagree   d. strongly disagree

20. I feel that successful students perceive their instructors as experts.
    a. strongly agree   b. agree   c. disagree   d. strongly disagree

21. Successful students stick to an organized study routine.
    a. strongly agree   b. agree   c. disagree   d. strongly disagree

22. Successful students develop a collection of study-skills strategies.
    a. strongly agree   b. agree   c. disagree   d. strongly disagree

23. Successful students take responsibility for their own learning.
    a. strongly agree   b. agree   c. disagree   d. strongly disagree

24. I am comfortable using the computer and searching the Internet.
    a. strongly agree   b. agree   c. disagree   d. strongly disagree

25. Learning to evaluate information on the World Wide Web is a priority for me.
    a. strongly agree   b. agree   c. disagree   d. strongly disagree

24. How many books have you read in your lifetime?
    a. none   b. 1-5   c. 5-10   d. too many to count

25. How many hours of TV do you watch per day?
    a. none   b. 1-2   c. 3-5   d. too many to count

Introduction Bingo

Circulate around the room and acquire the signature of anyone who can accurately fit the descriptions below. You may not use anyone's name more than once. Be sure to have the person sign your sheet in the appropriate box.

Someone with a highlighter	Someone who can name the author of *The Brethren, The Partner,* and *The Client*	Someone who is a visual learner	Someone who can name three attributes of an active learner	Someone with a dictionary
Someone who can name three attributes of an effective instructor	Someone who is an auditory learner	Someone who can change a flat tire without reading instructions	Someone who color-codes notes	Someone with a thesaurus
Someone who learns best by listening, rather than taking notes	Someone who knows who was in the trunk in the Dixie Chicks' song	Someone who knows the deadline to withdraw with a grade of *w*	Someone who can explain the first-aid term RICE	Someone who is a kinesthetic learner
Someone who uses Instant Messenger daily	Someone who reads to his or her child each night	Someone who reads at least 15 minutes each day	Someone who can describe an urban legend	Someone who can name five kinds of information that you can find on the Internet for free
Someone who listens to music when he or she studies	Someone who doodles in his or her notebook	Someone who needs to walk around when he or she reads	Someone who exercises regularly	Someone who watches people and studies body language

Part V: Answer Keys

PART ONE: A HANDBOOK FOR READING AND THINKING IN COLLEGE ANSWER KEY

Chapter 1 – Active Reading and Thinking Strategies

Section 1a

Active Reading (p. 4)

1. annotate as you read, compare and contrast the poems' subject matter, language, and meaning
2. underline key steps, visualize the process, focus on overall purpose of the lab
3. underline, write summary notes, discover how the article relates to course content

Section 1b

What Did You Learn from Previewing? (p. 8)

1. T
2. T
3. F
4. F
5. T

Now Practice Previewing (p. 9-14)

1. animal emotions
2. Answers will vary.
   a. cats
   b. polar bears
   c. orangutans
   d. whales
3. Answers will vary.
   a. happiness
   b. joy
   c. mourning
4. Answers will vary.

Section 1d

Now Practice Checking Your Comprehension (p. 15-16)

1. Answers will vary.
2. Answers will vary.
3. Answers will vary.
4. Answers will vary.
5. Answers will vary.

Chapter 2 – Vocabulary Building

Section 2a

Now Practice Using Definition Clues 1 (p. 20)

1. frankness of expression
2. a strong attractive force that holds atoms together
3. sense of hearing
4. group of animal or plants that share similar characteristics and are able to interbreed
5. periods of time between an infection and appearance of a symptom

Now Practice Using Definition Clues 2 (p. 20-21)

1. the period of growth from childhood to maturity
2. small, closely knit groups of friends who spend most or all of their time together
3. individuals who have friends from several cliques but belong to none
4. individuals with few friends
5. loose associations of cliques that usually meet on weekends

Now Practice Using Example Clues 1 (p. 22)

1. reserved; restrained
2. information about performance or results
3. materials
4. natural, necessary, unconscious bodily activities

5. words with identical pronunciations but different spellings

Now Practice Using Example Clues 2 (p. 22-23)
1. a lake zone near the shore in which abundant light and nutrients support a diverse plant and animal community
2. photosynthesizing, microscopic organisms present in a lake's littoral zone
3. nonphotosynthesizing, microscopic organisms present in a lake's littoral zone
4. an open-water lake zone that allows enough light for photosynthesis; it is inhabited by bacteria, zooplankton, crustaceans, and fish
5. a deep, dark lake zone that does not support photosynthesis; it is inhabited by decomposers, detritus feeders, and fish

Now Practice Using Contrast Clues 1 (p. 24)
1. wealthy; well-to-do
2. doubtful
3. agreed
4. condemned; spoke against
5. renovated; changed; updated

Now Practice Using Contrast Clues 2 (p. 24- 25)
1. misleading, deceptive
2. living in luxury, indulging in fancy tastes
3. rejects, turns away from
4. modest, plain, simple
5. someone from high society, far from the "common man"

Now Practice Using Logic of the Passage Clues 1 (p. 25-26)
1. incorporated; absorbed
2. financially supported
3. place of safety
4. frightened; deterred
5. future emergency

Now Practice Using Logic of the Passage Clues 2 (p. 26)
1. b. unchanging
2. a. spreading
3. c. supporters
4. a. communication
5. c. language held in common by many countries

Section 2b
Now Practice Using Prefixes 1(p. 29)
1. bi
2. sub
3. im
4. ir
5. mis
6. multi
7. inter
8. dis
9. sub
10. retro

Now Practice Using Prefixes 2 (p. 31)
1. uni
2. bi
3. pseudo
4. sub
5. multi

Now Practice Using Roots 1 (p. 33-34)
1. a duplicate copy or reproduction
2. ability to be seen
3. written evidence of one's qualifications

4. to guess, reflect, take a risk
5. a tract of land; the character or quality of land
6. a trial or hearing; a presentation of something heard
7. a study of the physics of the stars
8. a record of events in time order or sequence
9. a person's signature

Now Practice Using Roots 2 (p. 34)
1. photo
2. scope
3. logy
4. mit
5. astro

Now Practice Using Suffixes 1 (p. 37-38)
1. conversation
2. assistant
3. qualifications
4. internship
5. eaten
6. audible
7. seasonable
8. permission
9. instructive
10. memory

Now Practice Using Suffixes 2 (p. 38)
1. biologists
2. impassable
3. oceanic
4. geological
5. continuous

Chapter 3 – Thesis, Main Ideas, Supporting Details, and Transitions
Section 3a
Now Practice Identifying Thesis Statements (p. 40)
1. c
2. a
3. b
4. c

Section 3b
Now Practice Finding Main Ideas 1 (p.44-47)
1. Evidence suggests that groups given the right to vote do not immediately exercise that right.
2. The symbols that constitute language are commonly referred to as words—labels that we have assigned to concepts, or our mental representations.
3. One way to determine the amount of adipose tissue is to measure the whole-body density.
4. In other words, at least some of the behavior normally called instinct is partly learned.
5. These developments point to the continuing controversy over the impact of election-night coverage on voter turnout.
6. According to economic data, a tiny segment of the American population owns most of the nation's wealth.
7. As a conflict strategy, gunnysacking refers to the practice of storing up grievances so we may unload them at another time.
8. But e-mail also has its share of problems and pitfalls, including privacy.
9. Couvade refers to "a variety of customs applying to the behavior of fathers during the pregnancies of their wives and during and shortly after the births of their children."
10. Unless stated otherwise, when we discuss the speeds of things in our environment, we mean relative to the surface of the earth; motion is relative.

Now Practice Finding Main Ideas 2 (p. 47)
1. The meanings we impart to these symbols are largely influenced by our culture, so marketers need to take special care that the symbol they use in a foreign market has the meaning they intended.
2. For assistance in understanding how consumers interpret the meanings of symbols, some marketers are turning to a field of study known as semiotics, which examines how people assign meanings to symbols.
3. Marketers also need to be concerned about taboos and superstitions.

Now Practice Finding Main Ideas 3 (p. 48-49)
1. a
2. d
3. d
4. d
5. a

Section 3c
Now Practice Understanding Implied Main Ideas 1 (p. 50-53)
Paragraph A

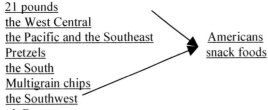

Paragraph B

Paragraph C

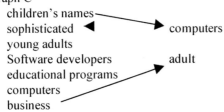

Now Practice Understanding Implied Main Ideas 2 (p. 53-55)
1. Changes in police work since 1960 have had mixed results.
2. It is difficult to estimate the value of a homemaker's services.
3. Since 1970, the penalties for drug dealing have increased.

Now Practice Understanding Implied Main Ideas 3 (p. 55-57)
1. d
2. c
3. a
4. c
5. c
6. b
7. a
8. c
9. a
10. c

226

Now Practice Finding Stated and Implied Main Ideas (p. 58)
1.—18.   Answers will vary.

Section 3d

Now Practice Finding Supporting Details 1 (p. 59-61)
1.   a
      b
      d
2.   a
      b
      e
3.   b
      c
      d
4.   b
      c
      d
      e
5.   b
      c
      d

Now Practice Finding Supporting Details 2 (p. 61-62)

1. *Tolerance* means that more and more of the drug must be taken to achieve the same effect, as use continues. *Withdrawal* means that if use is discontinued, the person experiences unpleasant symptoms.
2 .*Caffeine* is the active ingredient in coffee, tea, and many cola drinks. *Nicotine* is the active ingredient in tobacco.
3. In psychotherapy, it is most often used to eliminate bad habits and annoying symptoms. Sufferers of migraine headaches treated with hypnotic suggestions to relax showed a much greater tendency to improve than sufferers treated with drugs; 44 percent were headache-free after 12 months of treatment, compared to 12 percent of their drug-treated counterparts.
4. The traditional *absorptive* glasses soak up all the harmful sun rays. *Polarizing* sunglasses account for half the market. They're the best buy for knocking out glare, and reflections from snow and water, but they may admit more light rays than other sunglasses. *Coated* sunglasses usually have a metallic covering that itself reflects light. …*photochromatic* sunglasses. Their chemical composition causes them to change color according to the brightness of the light: in the sun, they darken; in the shade, they lighten.
5.… a candidate campaigns within his party for nomination at a national convention. … period of competition with the nominee of the other major party and perhaps the nominees of minor parties. The candidate must win more votes than any other nominee in enough states and the District of Columbia to give him a majority of the electoral votes. … President of the .

Now Practice Finding Supporting Details 3 (p.62)
Answers will vary.

Section 3e

Now Practice Recognizing Transitions 1(p. 63-64)
1.   Another
2.   however
3.   More important
4.   for example
5.   Because

Now Practice Recognizing Transitions 2 (p. 64-65)
1.   also
2.   because
3.   Next
4.   For example

227

5. Similarly
6. However
7. In addition/also
8. For example
9. After
10. On the other hand/however

Now Practice Recognizing Transitions 3 (p. 65)
1. e
2. g
3. j
4. a
5. i
6. h
7. c
8. d
9. b
10. f

Now Practice Recognizing Transitions 4 (p.66)
1. an example of the valuable services that pharmacies provide
2. one suggestion for preventing a home burglary
3. information that suggest some mail order businesses are not honest and reliable
4. a second advantage of a compact stereo system
5. the next step in choosing a candidate you will vote for

Now Practice Recognizing Transitions 5 (p.66)
1. Answers will vary.
2. Answers will vary.
3. Answers will vary.
4. Answers will vary.
5. Answers will vary.

Chapter 4 – Organizational Patterns

Section 4a
Now Practice Using Definition (p. 69-70)
1. pidgin
2. It is a language that develops when people who speak different languages live near one another.
3. Tok Pisin
4. It is the skin that covers the body.
5. waterproofs the body, protects tissue, excretes salts and urea, regulates body temperature, serves as a sensor for the body surface

Section 4b
Now Practice Using Classification (p. 71-72)
1. pterosaurs, archaeopteryx, plesiosaurs, and ichthyosaurs
2. One group, another group
3. spiral, elliptical, irregular
4. shape
5. several basic types, one type, are classified as

Section 4c
Now Practice Using Order or Sequence (p. 74-75)
1. railroad construction
2. The building of the railroads encouraged businesses to grow and develop.
3. Beginning in 1862, in 1869, by 1890
4. The events leading up to the bombing inside North Vietnam and the full-scale intervention in Vietnam.
5. in late July 1964, on July 30, simultaneously, on August 2, on August 3, although somewhat later

Now Practice Using Process (p. 76-77)
1. how Olestra creates the taste of fat without the calories
2. because the body cannot convert Olestra's molecules into sucrose and fatty acids and the molecules are

too large to enter the bloodstream undigested
3. the calculation of BMI
4. Divide your height in inches by 39.4, then square the result.
5. It measures the relationship of height and weight; it predicts health risks due to being overweight.

Now Practice Using Order of Importance (p. 78-79)
1. the three main types of resources that are currently important
2. first, the most important, second, finally
3. because of its reach and influence
4. advanced electronic mass media
5. Internet chat rooms, personalized Web pages

Now Practice Using Spatial Order (p. 80)
1. Skeletal tissue is tissue that is attached to bones and is voluntary
2. attached to, parallel, surrounding, near
3. The fibers are arranged parallel to each other.
4. They surround the saroplasm (or cytoplasm).
5. They are located near the sarcolemma.

Section 4d
Now Practice Using Cause and Effect (p. 82-83)
A. 1. All objects continue to absorb radiant energy, and some objects absorb more than they radiate.
    2. Its temperature will approach absolute zero.
    3. Why, therefore
    4. emitting as much radiant energy as it receives
    5. Its temperature will approach absolute zero.
B. 6. repetitive motion
    7. irritation to the median nerve in the wrist
    8. typing
    9. numbness, tingling and pain in the fingers or toes
   10. result from, result in

Section 4e
Now Practice Using Comparison and Contrast (p. 85-86)
1. Congress, presidency
2. contrast
3. Differences: constituencies from which elected, types of concerns expected to address, structure, speed of action, and unity
4. because Congress is composed of hundreds of people divided along party lines
5. basic differences, structural differences
6. postindustrial and industrial societies
7. information
8. produce things
9. People are willing to pay for information or services based on information.
10. unlike, rather, unlike, rather

Section 4f
Now Practice Using Listing (p. 87-88)
1. the characteristics of minority groups
2. They come into existence when, due to expanded boundaries or migration, people with different customs, languages, values, or physical characteristics come under the control of the same state organization.
3. the decisions voters make at election time and the factors that influence voter choice
4. two basic decisions, the first, second, three factors
5. Voter turnout is low due to the registration system.

Section 4g
Now Practice Using Organization Patterns 1 (p. 89-90)
1. comparison and contrast or cause and effect
2. cause and effect/definition
3. process or listing
4. definition

5. order or sequence
6. order of importance
7. cause and effect
8. spatial
9. comparison and contrast
10. listing/enumeration

Now Practice Using Organization Patterns 2 (p. 90-91)
1. order or sequence
2. classification/definition
3. process
4. listing/enumeration
5. comparison and contrast

Section 4h
Now Practice Using Organization Patterns 3 (p. 94-95)
1. statement and clarification
2. addition
3. generalization and example
4. summary
5. summary
6. statement and clarification
7. generalization and example

Now Practice Using Organization Patterns 4 (pp. 95-96)
1. generalization and example
2. statement and clarification
3. summary
4. addition
5. generalization and example

Chapter 5 – Making Inferences

Section 5a
Now Practice Making Inferences 1 (p. 100)
Answers will vary.
Now Practice Making Inferences 2 (p. 101)
1. b and d
2. a, b, and d
3. b, c, and d

Section 5c
Now Practice Making Inferences 3 (p. 104)
2 and 4
Now Practice Making Inferences 4 (p. 105)
1. a.
   b.
2. a.
   b.
   c.
3. b.

   d.
Now Practice Making Inferences 5 (p. 105-107)
1. b and c
2. a ,c, and d
3. a and d
Now Practice Making Inferences 6 (p. 107-108)
1. PA
2. IE
3. IE

4. PA
5. IE
6. PA
7. IE
8. PA
9. IE
10. IE
Now Practice Making Inferences 7 (p. 108-109)
    b, c, d, and f

Chapter 6 – Critical Reading

Section 6a

Now Practice Distinguishing Fact and Opinion 1 (p. 112)
1. F
2. O
3. F
4. O
5. EO
6. F
7. EO
8. EO
9. O
10. F

Now Practice Distinguishing Fact and Opinion 2 (p. 112 -114)
A. 1. fact
   2. opinion
   3. fact
   4. fact
   5. opinion
B. 1. fact
   2. opinion
   3. fact
   4. fact
   5. opinion
C. 1. fact
   2. opinion
   3. opinion
   4. fact
   5. opinion
D. 1. fact
   2. fact
   3. opinion
   4. fact
   5. opinion
E. 1. expert opinion
   2. fact
   3. fact
   4. fact
   5. opinion

Section 6b

Now Practice Identifying the Author's Purpose 1 (p. 115-116)
1. to advise
2. to entertain
3. to inform
4. to persuade

5. to criticize

Now Practice Identifying the Author's Purpose 2 (p. 116-117)
1. This was written for people with enough income to invest money.
2. This was written for environmentally conscious people who are concerned about their health.
3. This was written for teenagers who own cars.
4. This is intended for people who do laundry.
5. This is intended for car owners who are unfamiliar with a car's trouble signs and maintenance.

Section 6c

Now Practice Recognizing Tone 1 (p.118-119)
1. disapproving
2. informative
3. admiring
4. nostalgic
5. humorous
6. sarcastic
7. optimistic
8. cynical/bitter
9. excited
10. formal

Now Practice Recognizing Tone 2 (p.119-120)
1. The tone of this statement seems logical and persuasive.
   words: *scientific evidence; clear and obvious; at least as safe as*
2. The author of this statement is angry and disturbed.
   words: *outrageous; littered; unsafe; problems*
3. The author of this statement seems disgusted with the legal system.
   words: *tired; victims; hassled*
4. This statement is intended to be instructive.
   words: *different shapes and materials; Be sure that; on the ski right where*
5. The tone of this statement is one of deep emotion, conveying a feeling of tragedy and sorrow.
   words: *beautiful little girl; impossible to describe the effect; changed us*

Section 6d

Now Practice Detecting Bias 1 (p.122)
1, 3, 6, 8 and 9

Now Practice Detecting Bias 2 (p.122-123)
1. blot out
2. trip
3. put off
4. spend hour after hour

Section 6e

Now Practice Evaluating Data and Evidence (p.123-124)
1. examples
2. expert opinion
3. examples, expert opinion
4. research citation
5. expert opinion

Section 6f

Now Practice Using Connotative Language 1 (p.125
1. request
2. overlook
3. tease
4. display
5. gown
6. showy
7. artificial
8. costly
9. choosy

10. take

Now Practice Using Connotative Language 2 (p.125)
1. extensively
2. stiff
3. productive
4. persistent
5. risky

Now Practice Using Figurative Language 1 (p. 127-128)
1. a
2. b
3. c
4. d
5. b

Now Practice Using Figurative Language (p. 128-129)
1. A feather is light, whimsical, and blows away easily. The author is suggesting that hope is changeable and unsteady, undependable.
2. Spilled paint is messy and splotchy; it spreads fast and unevenly. The author is suggesting that the woman's blushed face was obvious and somewhat unattractive.
3. A powerboat uses money in a way similar to how a hungry animal eats food. A powerboat is a vehicle that requires a great deal of money to support.
4. Sally's skin was shiny and clear with a reflective quality.
5. The speaker destroyed her dreams in a sharp, deliberate, and forceful manner.

Chapter 7 – Organizing Ideas

Section 7a
Now Practice Highlighting 1 (p. 132-133)
Examples A and B
1. B
2. Example A contains too much highlighting. Too many details are highlighted, and the highlighting will not save much time in reviewing.
Examples C and D
1. C
2. Important key words and phrases are not highlighted in Example D.
Now Practice Highlighting 2 (p. 133)
    Answers will vary.

Section 7b
Now Practice Annotating 1 (p. 134)
    Answers will vary.
Now Practice Annotating 2 (p. 134)
    Answers will vary.

Section 7c
Now Practice Using Paraphrasing 1 (p. 136-137)
1. 2
2. Answers will vary. Paraphrase 1 does not contain the important idea that silence varies cross culturally. Paraphrase 3 is inaccurate (not all Siberian women are silent) and it does not explain that silence is a form of communication that varies cross-culturally. It does not explain that silence does not always indicate powerlessness.
3. 3
4. Paraphrase 1 does not contain enough information. Paraphrase 2 is inaccurate; it states the projected statistic as a fact.
Now Practice Using Paraphrasing 2 (p. 138)
    Answers will vary.

Section 7d
Now Practice Outlining 1 (p. 139-140)
A.
    2. aggressiveness, athleticism, being physically active, being logical, and dominance over females in

social relationships

B.

1. attributes society believes appropriate for females

2. passivity, docility, fragility, emotionality

C. Children   age 4

D.

2. aggression vary widely within the sexes and between them

Now Practice Outlining 2 (p. 140)

　Answers will vary.

Section 7e

Now Practice Drawing a Conceptual Map 1 (p. 141-142)

1. meeting

2. take over from older generation, keep society going

3. young to become contributors to welfare of society

4. Religious institutions; bearable or satisfying

5. makes and enforces laws to prevent destabilization of society

Now Practice Drawing a Conceptual Map 2 (p. 142)

　Answers will vary.

Now Practice Drawing a Process Diagram 1 (p. 143-144)

1. bill

2. vote

3. Senate

4. president

5. signs

6. 2/3 vote

7. does not pass

8. law, U.S. Criminal Codes

Now Practice Drawing a Process Diagram 2 (p. 145)

　Answers will vary.

Now Practice Drawing a Time Line (p.146)

　Answers will vary.

Now Practice Drawing a Part/Function Diagram (p. 147-148)

　Answers will vary.

Section 7f

Now Practice Summarizing 1 (p. 149)

Psychedelic drugs cause *hallucinations* and can cause reactions mimicking *mental disorders*. Examples include *mescaline, peyote, and psilocybin*. LSD is the best known and was most popular *in the late 1960s*. It is created from *lysergic acid,* which comes from a *fungus that lives on cereal grain*. Initially, it causes weakness, *dizzines, and nausea* and later a distortion of time and space. It causes the senses to be *stronger and mixed up with each other*. The drug affects *people's moods*, creates a feeling of distance, and creates changes *in self-perception*. The sensations resulting are outside *the normal range of experiences. Bad trips* can have *long-term* consequences and the reason for them is not understood.

Now Practice Summarizing 2 (p. 149)

　Answers will vary.

Chapter 8 – Improving And Adjusting Your Reading Rate

Section 8b

Now Practice Adjusting Your Reading Rate (p. 152-153)

1. Understand all clauses and aspects of the agreement or policy

　　　Comprehension level: complete

2. Analyze and interpret the sonnet

　　　Comprehension level: high

3. Obtain a general overview of the topic

　　　Comprehension level: moderate

4. Understand sequence and relationship of events; consider political implications
   Comprehension level: high
5. Note historical events; get a general sense of the times and the culture
   Comprehension Level: moderate

Chapter 9 – Reading And Evaluating Electronic Sources

Section 9a

Now Practice New Ways of Thinking and Reading 1 (p. 158)

1. http://www.consumer.gov
   1. Inspect the car carefully.
   2. Take the car for a test drive in traffic, on the open road, and up hills.
   3. Examine the repair and maintenance records for the car.
   4. Ask the previous owner about the car.
   5. Hire your own mechanic to look over the car.

2. http://ww.bls.gov.oco/
   There will be fewer opportunities.

3. http://thomas.loc.gov/home/lawsmade.toc.html
   The system of lights and ringing bells is used to inform members of Congress about certain events taking place in the House and Senate chambers while these members are away on other business in the Capitol building or office buildings.

Now Practice New Ways of Thinking and Reading 2 (p. 159)

1. Answers will vary.
2. Answers will vary.
3. Answers will vary.

Section 9c

Now Practice Evaluating Content (p. 162)

1. The site presents many good points about environmental conservation. However, it does not cite any sources or openly reveal the author's credentials. There are some broken links which need to be fixed.
2. The site is sponsored by the University of Minnesota. The site makes explicit statements that this is a tutorial only and explains clearly what the site will and will not do. All of the contributors are identified and contact information is provided.
3. This site makes very strong and biased claims, calling them "facts." No sources are provided for the data presented. More research would be necessary before using this site.

Now Practice Evaluating Accuracy (p. 163-164)

1. Complete credentials and contact information of experts on gun use are included. The mission and purpose are clear. There are no dates to use in verifying the information.
2. While this site may present actual real sections of the U.S. Tax Code, it is unclear as to whether or not the interpretation can be trusted. The author is not identified and no outside supporting references are made. The long explanation concludes with a solicitation.
3. Although the user may not realize it immediately, this site is for entertainment purposes only. Its "news" is based on real events, but then elaborated upon with humor and sarcasm.

Now Practice Evaluating Time Lines (p. 164)

1. This site contains many outdated links. It does not help a user keep up with the fast-changing Internet environment.
2. The article shown here is from almost ten years ago. Some of the information may still be useful, but without updates, the user cannot be sure of its value.
3. Answers will vary.

PART TWO: READINGS FOR ACADEMIC DISCIPLINES ANSWER KEY

Chapter 11 – Social Sciences

Selection 1 "Urban Legends"

Previewing the Reading

1. What are urban legends?

2. urban legends
A. Understanding the Thesis and Other Main Ideas
   1. d
   2. b
   3. b
   4. c
   5. b
B. Identifying Details
   1. c
   2. b
   3. d
   4. a
   5. a
C. Recognizing Methods of Organization and Transitions
   1. enumeration
   2. first
   3. second
   4. third
D. Reviewing and Organizing Ideas: Mapping
   The answers below appear from top to bottom and from left to right in the map.
   1. young people to be careful
   2. "Kentucky Fried Rat" warns people to eat at home
   3. "The Hook"
   4. changing male-female relationships
   5. "The Hook" instills fear of the dangerous unknown
   6. "Kentucky Fried Rat"
E. Figuring Out Inferred Meanings
   1. F
   2. T
   3. F
   4. F
   5. T
F. Thinking Critically
   1. a
   2. b
   3. c
   4. d
G. Building Vocabulary
   Context
   1. d
   2. a
   3. a
   Word Parts
   1. tens of years
   2. one who studies folklore
   3. the condition of sending across / communication
   4. the quality of believing / believability
   Unusual Words/Unusual Meanings
   1. b
H. Selecting a Learning/Study Strategy
   Answers will vary.
I. Exploring Ideas Through Discussion and Writing
   Answers will vary.
J. Beyond the Classroom to the Web
   Answers will vary.

Selection 2 "The New Flirting Game"

Previewing the Reading
    1. flirting
    2. a. What is the "flirting game"? or Why do people flirt?
        b. Who takes the lead in flirting?
        c. What are sexual semaphores? or Who is submissive in flirting?

A.   Understanding the Thesis and Other Main Ideas
    1. d
    2. d
    3. a
    4. c
    5. d
    6. a
    7. b

B.   Identifying Details
    1. c
    2. b
    3. d
    4. c
    5. c
    6. c

C.   Recognizing Methods of Organization and Transitions
    1. For instance
    2. comparison and contrast, Compared with adults

D.   Reviewing and Organizing Ideas: Paraphrasing
    1. ethologists
    2. signs
    3. submissiveness
    4. behaviors
    5. courtship
    6. powerful
    7. covering your mouth
    8. submissive
    9. baring the neck
    10. erogenous zone
    11. submissive
    12. sample
    13. coy smile
    14. direct eye contact
    15. smiled

E.   Figuring Out Inferred Meanings
    1. T
    2. F
    3. F
    4. F
    5. T

F.   Thinking Critically
    1. b
    2. d
    3. c
    4. d
    5. a

G.   Building Vocabulary
   Context
    1. b
    2. d

3. a
4. a
5. b
6. d
Word Parts
1. d
2. e
3. f
4. a
5. c
6. b
Unusual Words/Unusual Meanings
1. T
2. T
H. Selecting a Learning/Study Strategy
Answers will vary.
I. Exploring Ideas Through Discussion and Writing
Answers will vary.
J. Beyond the Classroom to the Web
Answers will vary.

Selection 3 "Coming into My Own"

Previewing the Reading
1. A hospital
2. A medical doctor
A. Understanding the Thesis and Other Main Ideas
1. c
2. c
3. a
4. a
5. b
6. d
B. Identifying Details
1. T
2. F
3. F
4. F
5. T
C. Recognizing Methods of Organization and Transitions
1. b
2. c
D. Reviewing and Organizing Ideas: Summarizing
1. respiratory therapist
2. doctor
3. past experiences
4. white
5. black
6. complained/protested
7. they could either leave or stay and be treated by a black doctor
8. laughed
9. prejudices
10. prejudice based on color or ethnic background
E. Figuring Out Inferred Meanings
1. F
2. T
3. F

F. Thinking Critically
    1. b
    2. a
    3. b
    4. c
G. Building Vocabulary
    Context
    1. b
    2. c
    3. a
    4. b
    Word Parts
    1. d
    2. b
    3. c
    Unusual Words/Unusual Meanings
    1. Answers will vary.
    2. Answers will vary.
H. Selecting a Learning/Study Strategy
    Answers will vary.
I. Exploring Ideas Through Discussion and Writing
    Answers will vary.
J. Beyond the Classroom to the Web
    Answers will vary.

Chapter 12 – Communication/Speech
Selection 4 "Reality TV: Race to the Bottom"

Previewing the Reading
1. reality TV
2. Big Brother, Survivor, The Bachelor, Paradise Hotel
3. profanity, explicit language, graphic content
A. Understanding the Thesis and Other Main Ideas
    1. d
    2. a
    3. b
    4. c
    5. b
B. Identifying Details
    1. F
    2. T
    3. T
    4. T
    5. F
C. Recognizing Methods of Organization and Transitions
    1. also, but
    2. comparison/contrast
D. Reviewing and Organizing Ideas: Summarizing
    1. scripted
    2. behavior
    3. reality
    4. irresponsible
    5. dangerous
    6. Networks
    7. offensive
    8. Sponsors

9. producers
10. FCC
11. decency
E. Figuring Out Inferred Meanings
   1. T
   2. F
   3. F
   4. T
   5. T
F. Thinking Critically
   1. a
   2. d
   3. b
   4. a
   5. a
G. Building Vocabulary
   Context
   1. a
   2. a
   3. c
   4. a
   Word Parts
   1. through
   2. between
   3. apart
   Unusual Words/Unusual Meanings
   1. Answers will vary.
   2. Answers will vary.
   3. Answers will vary.
H. Selecting a Learning/Study Strategy
   1. d
I. Exploring Ideas Through Discussion and Writing
   Answers will vary.
J. Beyond the Classroom to the Web
   Answers will vary.

Selection 5 "War: The Mother of All Words"
Previewing the Reading
   1. war-related words becoming part of the language
   2. a. weapons-grade
      b. kamikazes
      c. grunts
      d. Ground Zero, snafu, basket case
A. Understanding the Thesis and Other Main Ideas
   1. b
   2. a
   3. d
   4. b
   5. a
   6. d
   7. a
   8. a
B. Identifying Details
   1. b
   2. d

3. a
4. e
5. c

C. Recognizing Methods of Organization and Transitions
1. a
2. b
3. c
4. b
5. d
6. c

D. Reviewing and Organizing Ideas: Paraphrasing
1. editors
2. include
3. Joseph Pickett
4. American Heritage
5. disappear
6. dictionary
7. absurd
8. years

E. Figuring Out Inferred Meanings
1. T
2. F
3. T
4. F
5. F

F. Thinking Critically
1. c
2. b
3. c
4. c
5. d
6. b
7. a

G. Building Vocabulary
Context
1. c
2. a
3. b
4. d
5. c
6. b

Word Parts
1. not
2. one who
3. above
4. all
5. four

Unusual Words/Unusual Meanings
1. Answers will vary.
2. Answers will vary.
3. Answers will vary.
4. Answers will vary.

H. Selecting a Learning/Study Strategy
Answers will vary.

I. Exploring Ideas Through Discussion and Writing
Answers will vary.

Selection 6 "Lovers"

Previewing the Reading
1.   types of love
2.   a.   Eros, Pragma
     b.   Ludos, Mania
     c.   Storge, Agape
A.   Understanding the Thesis and Other Main Ideas
1.   b
2.   c
3.   c
4.   d
5.   a
6.   d
B.   Identifying Details
1.   S
2.   L
3.   E
4.   A
5.   M
6.   P
C.   Recognizing Methods of Organization and Transitions
1.   b
2.   c
D.   Reviewing and Organizing Ideas: Mapping
Paragraph 6 Map
The answers below appear from top to bottom and from left to right in the map.
1.   game
2.   partner
3.   controlled
4.   aggression
5.   fidelity
Paragraph 7 Map
The answers below appear from top to bottom and from left to right in the map.
1.   passion
2.   late
3.   companionable
4.   interests
5.   gradual
6.   slowly
E.   Figuring Out Inferred Meanings
1.   T
2.   T
3.   F
4.   F
F.   Thinking Critically
1.   d
2.   b
3.   c
4.   b
5.   d
G.   Building Vocabulary
Context
1.   b
2.   c

3. b
4. a
5. c
6. a
Word Parts
1. between
2. not
3. perfect
4. outside
H. Selecting a Learning/Study Strategy
1. d
H. Exploring Ideas Through Discussion and Writing
Answers will vary.
I. Beyond the Classroom to the Web
Answers will vary.

Chapter 13 – Anthropology
Selection 7 "To Love and to Cherish"
Previewing the Reading
1. religious wedding ceremonies
2. a. Sikh
   b. Catholic
   c. African Methodist Episcopal
   d. Hellenic Orthodox, Judaism, Islam
A. Understanding the Thesis and Other Main Ideas
1. d
2. c
3. b
4. c
5. b
B. Identifying Details
1. B
2. D
3. E
4. A
5. C
6. D
7. F
8. B
9. E
10. B
11. D
12. F
13. A
14. A
15. C
C. Recognizing Methods of Organization and Transitions
1. enumeration
2. comparison and contrast
D. Reviewing and Organizing Ideas: Summarizing
1. A. judge
   B. town hall
II. B. 2. the bond between bride and groom's families
   C. 1. around four times
      2. the religion

        3. a. physical
           b. mental
E. Figuring Out Inferred Meanings
    1. T
    2. F
    3. T
    4. F
    5. F
F. Thinking Critically
    1. O
    2. F
    3. O
    4. F
    5. F
    6. O
G. Building Vocabulary
    Context
    1. a
    2. b
    3. a
    4. c
    5. a
    Word Parts
    1. back
    2. before
    Unusual Words/Unusual Meanings
     Answers will vary.
G. Selecting a Learning/Study Strategy
     Answers will vary.
H. Exploring Ideas Through Discussion and Writing
     Answers will vary.
I. Beyond the Classroom to the Web
     Answers will vary.

Selection 8 "Peti's Malu: Traditions of Samoan Tattooing"

Previewing the Reading
    1. the art of Samoan tattooing
    2. a. What traditions are part of Samoan tattooing? What is the history of tattooing in Samoa?
        b. Who is tattooed? For what reasons? How are females and males tattooed differently?
        c. How is the tattooist regarded in Samoa?
A. Understanding the Thesis and Other Main Ideas
    1. d
    2. b
    3. c
    4. a
    5. a
B. Identifying Details
    1. T
    2. T
    3. F
    4. T
    5. F
    6. F
C. Recognizing Methods of Organization and Transitions
    1. Soon
    2. now

3. From time to time
4. After a little more than two hours/ a while
D. Reviewing and Organizing Ideas: Mapping
Female Tattoos
1. giving birth
2. thighs
3. thin lines
4. four or five hours
Male tattoos
1. boyhood to manhood
2. knees
3. large areas
4. three days
5. one or two months
E. Figuring Out Inferred Meanings
1. F
2. T
3. F
4. T
5. F
6. T
F. Thinking Critically
1. d
2. b
3. c
4. d
5. c
6. a
G. Building Vocabulary
Context
1. b
2. c
3. d
4. b
Word Parts
1. one who
2. half
Unusual Words/Unusual Meanings
Answers will vary.
H. Selecting a Learning/Study Strategy
Answers will vary.
I. Exploring Ideas Through Discussion and Writing
Answers will vary.
J. Beyond the Classroom to the Web
Answers will vary.

Selection 9 "Play, Leisure, and Culture"
Previewing the Reading
1. fun or leisure
2. a. What is the difference between play and leisure?
   b. How do play and leisure differ in different cultures?

A. Understanding the Thesis and Other Main Ideas
1. c
2. a
3. a

4. c
B. Identifying Details
1. T
2. T
3. T
4. F
5. F
6. F
7. T
8. T
9. F
10. T
C. Recognizing Methods of Organization and Transitions
1. a
2. d
D. Reviewing and Organizing Ideas: Summarizing
1. non-Western
2. religion
3. spirituality
4. martial arts
5. self-control
6. concentration
7. India
8. wrestling
9. families
10. dedication
11. Hindu
12. yoga
13. diet
14. controlled self
15. moral
16. physical
E. Figuring Out Inferred Meanings
1. T
2. T
3. F
4. T
5. F
6. T
7. F
F. Thinking Critically
1. c
2. c
3. b
4. d
G. Building Vocabulary
Context
1. b
2. a
3. c
4 a
Word Parts
1. under
2. human beings
Unusual Words/Unusual Meanings
Answers will vary.

246

H. Selecting a Learning/Study Strategy
   Answers will vary.
I. Exploring Ideas Through Discussion and Writing
   Answers will vary.
J. Beyond the Classroom to the Web
   Answers will vary.

Chapter 14: Education
Selection 10 "Should Students Attend School Year Round? Yes"
Previewing the Reading
   1. year-round schooling
   2. a. What is the tradition of the ten-month year?
      d. What are the keys to year-round success?
      e. Is it time for a new tradition?/What would be the new tradition?
A. Understanding the Thesis and Other Main Ideas
   1. c
   2. a
   3. d
   4. b
   5. d
   6. b
B. Identifying Details
   1. T
   2. F
   3. T
   4. F
   5. F
C. Recognizing Methods of Organization and Transitions
   1. b
   2. a
   3. c
D. Reviewing and Organizing Ideas: Mapping
   The answers appear from top to bottom and from left to right in the map.
   1. agricultural
   2. ten months
   3. summer
   4. 180
   5. Teacher's
   6. institutions
   7. cost-effective
   8. forgetfulness
   9. students
   10. intersessions
E. Figuring Out Inferred Meanings
   1. T
   2. F
   3. F
   4. T
   5. F
F. Thinking Critically
   1. d
   2. b
   3. c
   4. d
   5. c

6. a
7. b
8. b
G. Building Vocabulary
Context
1. c
2. a
3. c
4. b
5. a
6. d
Word Parts
1. intersessions, between
2. reconfigure, again
Unusual Words/Unusual Meanings
Answers will vary.
H. Selecting a Learning/Study Strategy
Answers will vary.
I. Exploring Ideas Through Discussion and Writing
Answers will vary.
J. Beyond the Classroom to the Web
Answers will vary.

Selection 11 "Should Students Attend School Year Round? No"

Previewing the Reading
1. No
2. a. What questions should parents and taxpayers ask about year-round schools?
   b. How will summer heat affect year-round schools?
A. Understanding the Thesis and Other Main Ideas
1. c
2. a
3. a
4. a
5. d
6. d
B. Identifying Details
1. F
2. T
3. F
4. T
5. T
C. Recognizing Methods of Organization and Transitions
1. b
2. b
3. b
D. Reviewing and Organizing Ideas: Paraphrasing
1. school districts
2. tutoring
3. programs
4. budget
5. air-conditioned
6. education
7. improvement
8. review time
9. break
10. school programs

248

11. standards
E. Figuring Out Inferred Meanings
    1. Y
    2. Y
    3. N
    4. N
    5. N
    6. N
    7. Y
    8. Y
F. Thinking Critically
    1. b
    2. c
    3. d
    4. a
    5. b
G. Building Vocabulary
   Context
    1. c
    2. a
    3. c
    4. b
    5. b
    6. d
    7. b
    8. c
    9. a
    10. b
   Word Parts
    1. e
    2. a
    3. c
    4. d
    5. b
    6. f
   Unusual Words/Unusual Meanings
    1. Answers will vary.
    2. Answers will vary.
    3. Answers will vary.
    4. Answers will vary.
H. Selecting a Learning/Study Strategy
   b
I. Exploring Ideas Through Discussion and Writing
   Answers will vary.
J. Beyond the Classroom to the Web
   Answers will vary.

Selection 12 "His Name Is Michael: A Lesson on the Voices We Unknowingly Silence"
Previewing the Reading
    1. teacher, David
    2. What is the meaning of the title?
A. Understanding the Thesis and Other Main Ideas
    1. b
    2. c

3. c
4. a
5. d
6. a
B. Identifying Details
1. Paragraph 2
    1. 43
    2. 5-9
    3. progressive
    4. child-directed
    5. meaning-driven
    6. responsive
    7. assessment
2. Paragraphs 7-9
    1. moved away
    2. a month
    3. David
C. Recognizing Methods of Organization and Transitions
1. d
2. a
3. d
4. c
D. Reviewing and Organizing Ideas: Summarizing
I. A. 1. Michael
      2. bus rider
      3. speak English
  B. 2. classroom
     4. buddies
III. Bilingual
  A. informal observation
  B. Miguel
E. Figuring Out Inferred Meanings
1. T
2. T
3. F
4. F
5. T
6. F
7. T
8. T
F. Thinking Critically
1. b
2. c
3. d
4. d
5. c
6. d
G. Building Vocabulary
Context
1. b
2. a
3. b
4. c
5. c
6. d
7. a

8. b
9. c
10. a
Word Parts
1. wrongly or incorrectly
2. two languages
3. many
Unusual Words/Unusual Meanings
Answers will vary.
H. Selecting a Learning/Study Strategy
Answers will vary.
I. Exploring Ideas Through Discussion and Writing
Answers will vary.
J. Beyond the Classroom to the Web
Answers will vary.

Chapter 15 Arts/Humanities/Literature
Selection 13 " Shaping Her People's Heritage: Nampeyo (1852-1942)"
Previewing the Reading
1. Native American
2. pottery
3. late 1800s/early 1900s
A. Understanding the Thesis and Other Main Ideas
1. b
2. d
3. a
4. a
5. d
B. Identifying Details
1. b
2. d
3. b
4. b
5. d
C. Recognizing Methods of Organization and Transitions
1. b
2. c
D. Reviewing and Organizing Ideas: Mapping
The answers below appear from top to bottom and from left to right in the timeline.
1. Nampeyo
2. Hano
3. make pottery
4. Mid-1890s
5. Fewkes
6. Hopi
7. 1920s
8. eyesight
9. husband
10. Arts and Crafts
11. 1942
12. great granddaughters
E. Figuring Out Inferred Meanings
1. F
2. T
3. F

4. F
5. T
F. Thinking Critically
1. b
2. b
3. a
4. c
5. b
6. a
7. c
G. Building Vocabulary
Context
1. b
2. c
3. a
4. d
5. a
6. b
7. c
8. d
Word Parts
1. human beings
2. characteristic of
3. a person who, ancient or past
H. Selecting a Learning/Study Strategy
Answers will vary.
I. Exploring Ideas Through Discussion and Writing
Answers will vary.
J. Beyond the Classroom to the Web
Answers will vary.

Selection 14 "Gregory"

Previewing the Reading
1. Answers will vary, but may include, Why was the prisoner ordered to be shot?
2. Did the soldier shoot the prisoner?
3. How did the prisoner save the soldier's life?
A. Understanding the Thesis and Other Main Ideas
1. d
2. c
B. Identifying Details
1. b
2. a
3. a
4. d
5. c
6. a
C. Recognizing Methods of Organization and Transitions
1. b
2. the day before, during
3. first time, second time, etc.
4. that very morning
5. very first day
D. Reviewing and Organizing Ideas: Summarizing
1. Gregory
2. Maria

    3. left

    4. second-hand

    5. beautiful

    6. garden

    7. together

    8. jealous

    9. happy

E.   Figuring Out Inferred Meanings

    1. T

    2. T

    3. F

    4. F

    5. T

    6. T

    7. T

    8. T

F.   Thinking Critically

    1. a

    2. b

    3. d

    4. c

G. Building Vocabulary

    Context

    1. a

    2. d

    3. d

    4. a

    Word Parts

    1. example

    2. a long distance

    Unusual Words/Unusual Meanings

    Answers will vary.

H. Selecting a Learning/Study Strategy

    Answers will vary.

I.   Exploring Ideas Through Discussion and Writing

    Answers will vary.

J.   Beyond the Classroom to the Web

    Answers will vary.

Selection 15 "The Truth Is"

Previewing the Reading

    1. a. She has one Chickasaw hand and one white hand.

        b. She sleeps in a twin bed.

        c. Her pockets are empty.

A. Understanding the Thesis and Other Main Ideas

    1. c

    2. a

    3. b

    4. c

    5. a

B. Identifying Details

    1. c

    2. a

    3. d

    4. a

C. Recognizing Methods of Organization and Transitions

        1. a
        2. d
    D. Reviewing and Organizing Ideas: Mapping
        Possible Answers: is concerned about her identity, has been in love, wants amnesty, half-white, feels
        conflict, does not value material goods
    E. Figuring Out Inferred Meanings
        1. F
        2. F
        3. T
        4. F
        5. T
    F. Thinking Critically
        1. c
        2. b
        3. b
        4. a
        5. a
        6. d
        7. d
        8. d
        9. a
    G. Selecting a Learning/Study Strategy
        Answers will vary.
    H. Exploring Ideas Through Discussion and Writing
        Answers will vary.
    I. Beyond the Classroom to the Web
        Answers will vary.

Chapter 16 – Public Policy/Contemporary Issues
Selection 16 "The Effects of the Minimum Wage"
Previewing the Reading
        1. the lowest hourly wage which firms can legally pay workers
        2. a. What will be the effects of raising the minimum wage?
            b. Why is the minimum wage controversial?
    A. Understanding the Thesis and Other Main Ideas
        1. b
        2. a
        3. a
        4. b
        5. b
    B. Identifying Details
        1. F
        2. T
        3. T
        4. T
        5. F
    C. Recognizing Methods of Organization and Transitions
        1. Paragraph 3
            a. 5
            b. 1
            c. 3
            d. 2
            e. 4
        2. a. order of importance
            b. statement and clarification

      c. comparison and contrast

      d. generalization and example

      e. addition

D. Reviewing and Organizing Ideas: Summarizing

1. Paragraph 2
    1. support
    2. families
    3. earnings
    4. little
    5. minimum wage
    6. teens
    7. dependents
    8. making it harder to get jobs
    9. skills

2. Paragraph 8
    1. lose work
    2. job skills
    3. on-the-job training
    4. teen unemployment
    5. Thirty percent
    6. minority teens

E. Figuring Out Inferred Meanings
    1. T
    2. T
    3. F
    4. F
    5. T

F. Thinking Critically
    1. d
    2. b
    3. c
    4. a
    5. a

G. Building Vocabulary

Context
    1. b
    2. d
    3. d
    4. a
    5. c
    6. b
    7. c

Word Parts
    1. in favor of
    2. not important
    3. does not have money, opportunities, or resources

Unusual Words/Unusual Meanings

Answers will vary.

H. Selecting a Learning/Study Strategy

    1. b

I. Exploring Ideas Through Discussion and Writing

Answers will vary.

J. Beyond the Classroom to the Web

Answers will vary.

255

Selection 17 "When Living Is a Fate Worse Than Death"

Previewing the Reading
1. dying
2. hospital

A. Understanding the Thesis and Other Main Ideas
1. d
2. b
3. c
4. d
5. a

B. Identifying Details
1. T
2. F
3. F
4. T
5. F
6. F
7. T

C. Recognizing Methods of Organization and Transitions
1. a
2. b

D. Reviewing and Organizing Ideas: Paraphrasing
1. hospital
2. home
3. emergency room
4. nursing homes
5. 16
6. death
7. doctors
8. weaker
9. death
10. parents
11. ICUs
12. family
13. staff
14. machines
15. death

E. Figuring Out Inferred Meanings
1. T
2. T
3. F
4. T
5. F

F. Thinking Critically
1. d
2. b
3. c
4. b
5. c
6. d
7. d

G. Building Vocabulary
Context
1. b
2. b
3. c

4. b
Word Parts
1. abnormally or wrongly formed
2. above
3. therapist
H. Selecting a Learning/Study Strategy
    1. a
I. Exploring Ideas Through Discussion and Writing
    Answers will vary.
J. Beyond the Classroom to the Web
    Answers will vary.

Selection 18 "Seoul Searching"

Previewing the Reading
    1. the search for the birth mother of the author's adopted daughter
    2. Seoul, Korea
A. Understanding the Thesis and Other Main Ideas
    1. a
    2. d
    3. a
    4. b
    5. a
    6. c
    7. d
B. Identifying Details
    1. T
    2. F
    3. F
    4. F
    5. F
C. Recognizing Methods of Organization and Transitions
    1. b
    2. d
D. Reviewing and Organizing Ideas: Mapping
    1. 2
    2. 1
    3. 4
    4. 5
    5. 3
E. Figuring Out Inferred Meanings
    1. F
    2. F
    3. T
    4. T
    5. F
F. Thinking Critically
    1. d
    2. c
    3. c
    4. a
    5. d
    6. b
    7. c
G. Building Vocabulary
    Context

1. b
2. c
3. d
4. b
5. a
Word Parts
1. e
2. d
3. a
4. f
5. c
6. b
7. i
8. j
9. h
10. g
Unusual Words/Unusual Meanings
1. d
2. b
3. a
H. Selecting a Learning/Study Strategy
   Answers will vary.
I. Exploring Ideas Through Discussion and Writing
   Answers will vary.
J. Beyond the Classroom to the Web
   Answers will vary.

Chapter 17: Political Science/Government/ History
Selection 19 "The Beautiful Laughing Sisters—An Arrival Story"
Previewing the Reading
1. The journey of sisters from Iraq to America
2. a. Why did the family leave Iraq?
   b. Where did their journey take them?
   c. Where did they end up living in the ?
   d. How are they adjusting to life in America?
A. Understanding the Thesis and Other Main Ideas
   1. d
   2. b
   3. a
   4. d
   5. b
   6. d
   7. a
B. Identifying Details
   1. c
   2. a
   3. c
   4. d
   5. b
   6. a
   7. d
   8. c
   9. a
C. Recognizing Methods of Organization and Transitions
   1. b

2. a. Shireen was born in 1979.
    b. After Hussein came to power
    c. After that night
    d. One night
    e. Finally
D. Reviewing and Organizing Ideas: Outlining
    1. Lincoln
    2. jobs
    3. high school
    4. teachers
    5. students
    6. opportunities
    7. futures
    8. clothes
    9. makeup
    10. rights
E. Figuring Out Inferred Meanings
    1. T
    2. F
    3. T
    4. F
    5. F
F. Thinking Critically
    1. c
    2. d
    3. a
    4. a
    5. a
    6. c
    7. c
    8. d
    9. d
J. Building Vocabulary
    Context
    1. c
    2. c
    3. d
    4. c
    5. b
    Word Parts
    1. counted
    2. believe
    Unusual Words/Unusual Meanings
    Answers will vary.
K. Selecting a Learning/Study Strategy
    Make notes on the reading, paying particular attention to the problems this family experienced.
L. Exploring Ideas Through Discussion and Writing
    Answers will vary.
M. Beyond the Classroom to the Web
    Answers will vary.

Selection 20 "Profile of a Terrorist"
Previewing the Reading
    1. terrorists
    2. a. What types of terrorists are there?
       b. What are the characteristics of terrorists?

259

c. Why is it important to know about the different types of terrorists?

A. Understanding the Thesis and Other Main Ideas
    1. b
    2. a
    3. d
    4. b
    5. c
    6. a

B. Identifying Details
    1. c
    2. a
    3. c
    4. a
    5. b

C. Recognizing Methods of Organization and Transitions
    1. Classification
        Paragraph 3: Frederick Hacker suggested three categories
        Paragraph 5: Let us consider the three categories of terrorists
    2. comparison and contrast
        Paragraph 6: on the other hand
        Paragraph 8: the distinction between

D. Reviewing and Organizing Ideas: Mapping
    Types: Crazy, Criminal, Crusader
    Who needs to know? Officials
    Why? Prevent, terrorists

E. Figuring Out Inferred Meanings
    1. F
    2. T
    3. T
    4. F
    5. T

F. Thinking Critically
    1. c
    2. a
    3. d
    4. d
    5. b
    6. d

G. Building Vocabulary
    Context
    1. d
    2. a
    3. b
    4. c
    5. c
    6. c
    7. a
    Word Parts
    1. across
    2. away

H. Selecting a Learning/Study Strategy
    1. d

I. Exploring Ideas Through Discussion and Writing
    Answers will vary.

J. Beyond the Classroom to the Web
    Answers will vary.

Selection 21 "Whether to Vote: A Citizen's First Choice"

Previewing the Reading

    1. voting in American elections

    2. a. civic duty

       b. to support the democratic process

A. Understanding the Thesis and Other Main Ideas

    1. d

    2. a

    3. b

    4. d

    5. b

    6. c

B. Identifying Details

    1. c

    2. b

    3. a

    4. d

    5. c

    6. a

    7. a

    8. c

C. Recognizing Methods of Organization and Transitions

    1. c

    2. d

D. Reviewing and Organizing Ideas: Summarizing

    1. 1800: property-owning, white males, 21

    2. 1896: 80%, highest level

    3. 1998: Oregon, mail

    4. 2000: work, unable

    5. 2000: Florida, small number

    6. 2004: 100 million

E. Figuring Out Inferred Meanings

    1. T

    2. T

    3. F

    4. T

    5. T

F. Thinking Critically

    1. d

    2. c

    3. c

    4. a

    5. b

    6. c

G. Building Vocabulary

Context

    1. d

    2. a

    3. b

    4. d

    5. c

    6. a

Word Parts

    1. move into

    2. into

3. computers
Unusual Words/Unusual Meanings
Answers will vary.
H. Selecting a Learning/Study Strategy
    b
I. Exploring Ideas Through Discussion and Writing
    Answers will vary.
J. Beyond the Classroom to the Web
    Answers will vary.

Chapter 18 – Business/Advertising/Economics
Selection 22 "Four Simple Words That Guarantee the Job of Your Dreams"
Previewing the Reading
1. right place/right time
2. jobs

A. Understanding the Thesis and Other Main Ideas
1. d
2. c
3. a
4. b
5. d

B. Identifying Details
7. F
8. T
9. F
10. T
11. T

C. Recognizing Methods of Organization and Transitions
1. d
2. a
3. Let me explain
4. for instance

D. Reviewing and Organizing Ideas: Paraphrasing
Paragraphs 1-2
a. four
b. exasperating
c. friend
d. best job
e. responsibilities
f. suit
g. hours
h. congenial
i. future
j. promotions
k. how
l. job
m. reply
n. guesses
o. right place
p. right time

E. Figuring Out Inferred Meanings
1. P
2. N
3. N
4. P

5. P
6. N
7. P
8. N
9. P
F. Thinking Critically
   1. a
   2. b
   3. d
   4. c
G. Building Vocabulary
   Context
   1. b
   2. a
   3. a
   4. d
   5. c
   6. b
   Word Parts
   1. statistician
   2. unrealistic, not practical, impractical
   Unusual Words/Unusual Meanings
   1. f
   2. d
   3. a
   4. e
   5. b
H. Selecting a Learning/Study Strategy
   Answers will vary.
I. Exploring Ideas Through Discussion and Writing
   Answers will vary.
J. Beyond the Classroom to the Web
   Answers will vary.

Selection 23 "McDonald's Makes a Lot of People Angry for a Lot of Different Reasons"

Previewing the Reading
   1. How or why does McDonald's make people angry?
   2. a. nutrition environment
      b. advertising, employment
      c. animals, expansion
      d. free speech, capitalism
A. Understanding the Thesis and Other Main Ideas
   1. d
   2. c
   3. a
   4. d
   5. a
   6. b
   7. c
B. Identifying Details
   1. T
   2. F
   3. T
   4. T

5.   F
C.   Recognizing Methods of Organization and Transitions
1.   comparison and contrast
2.   comparison and contrast
3.   however
D.   Reviewing and Organizing Ideas: Outlining
1.   market
2.   standardized
3.   production line
4.   maximum turnover
5.   profits
6.   one million
7.   unemployed
8.   destroyer
9.   low
10.   local food outlets
11.   vulnerable
12.   Employee complaints
13.   rights
14.   Understaffing
15.   breaks
16.   illegal
17.   safety
18.   sewage
19.   dropped on the floor
20.   "McJobs"
21.   Trade unionists
22.   unionization attempts
23.   happy
24.   Problems
25.   third-party
26.   workers
27.   wages and conditions
E.   Figuring Out Inferred Meanings
1.   P
2.   P
3.   N
4.   N
5.   N
F.   Thinking Critically
1.   a
2.   c
3.   b
4.   c
G.   Building Vocabulary
Context
1.   c
2.   b
3.   a
4.   b
5.   a
6.   c
7.   d
Word Parts
1.   c
2.   d

264

3. e
4. b
5. a
Unusual Words/Unusual Meanings
1. b
2. c
H. Selecting a Learning/Study Strategy
Answers will vary.
I. Exploring Ideas Through Discussion and Writing
Answers will vary.
J. Beyond the Classroom to the Web
Answers will vary.

Selection 24 "Hispanic Americans: A Growing Market Segment"
Previewing the Reading
1. Hispanic Americans
2. a. What is the allure of the Hispanic market?
    b. What are Hispanic subcultures?
    c. What are some blunders that have been made in marketing to Hispanics?
    d. What is the Hispanic identity?
A. Understanding the Thesis and Other Main Ideas
    1. b
    2. c
    3. a
    4. d
    5. a
    6. d
B. Identifying Details
    1. a
    2. c
    3. b
    4. d
    5. b
    6. d
    7. b
    8. a
C. Recognizing Methods of Organization and Transitions
    1. enumeration
    2. First
    3. Second
    4. comparison and contrast
D. Reviewing and Organizing Ideas: Mapping
    The answers appear from top to bottom and from left to right in the map.
    1. for status
    2. of pride
    3. Self-expression
    4. Familial devotion
    5. Embarrassment in social situations
    6. Loss of control
    7. problem-solving
    8. Action-oriented
    9. Assertive role models in non-threatening situations
E. Figuring Out Inferred Meanings
    1. T
    2. T
    3. F

265

    4. F
    5. T
    6. T
F. Thinking Critically
    1. b
    2. c
    3. a
    4. d
    5. c
G. Building Vocabulary
    Context
    1. b
    2. c
    3. c
    4. c
    5. b
    6. a
    7. b
    8. d
    9. c
    Word Parts
    1. c
    2. e
    3. a
    4. b
    5. d
    6. g
    7. h
    8. f
    Unusual Words/Unusual Meanings
    1. Answers will vary.
    2. Answers will vary.
H. Selecting a Learning/Study Strategy
    1. b
I. Exploring Ideas Through Discussion and Writing
    Answers will vary.
J. Beyond the Classroom to the Web
    Answers will vary.

Chapter 19 – Technology/Computers
Selection 25 "Blogger Beware"
Previewing the Reading
    1. blogging
    2. workplace blogging, defamation, and international blogging
A. Understanding the Thesis and Other Main Ideas
    1. b
    2. c
    3. d
    4. a
    5. b
    6. a
B. Identifying Details
    1. images, links, discussion
    2. publication of private information, election-related activities, copyrighted or trademarked content
C. Recognizing Methods of Organization and Transitions

266

1. a
2. b
D. Reviewing and Organizing Ideas: Mapping
   Answers start at the top in clock-wise order.
   1. State and federal laws, "whistle blogging"
   2. political or social issues
   3. legal right, blogging
   4. at home
   5. company computers, software, e-mail
   6. legal problems
E. Figuring Out Inferred Meanings
   1. T
   2. T
   3. F
   4. T
   5. F
   6. T
F. Thinking Critically
   1. b
   2. d
   3. c
   4. c
G. Building Vocabulary
   Context
   1. b
   2. a
   3. c
   4. d
   5. c
   6. a
   7. a
   8. c
   9. b
   Word Parts
   1. jurisdiction
      tell or say, law
   2. person who writes blogs
      person who makes comments
   Unusual Words/Unusual Meanings
   1. latitude
      Answers will vary.
   2. tread in legally dangerous waters
      Answers will vary.
H. Selecting a Learning/Study Strategy
   Answers will vary.
I. Exploring Ideas Through Discussion and Writing
   Answers will vary.
J. Beyond the Classroom to the Web
   Answers will vary.

Selection 26 "Hold It Right There, and Drop That Camera"

Previewing the Reading
   1. camera phones
   2. a. lavatories
      b. dressing rooms
      c. locker rooms

267

A. Understanding the Thesis and Other Main Ideas
    1. d
    2. d
    3. c
    4. b
    5. a
B. Identifying Details
    1. b
    2. c
    3. d
    4. a
    5. a
C. Recognizing Methods of Organization and Transitions
    1. enumeration
    2. also
D. Reviewing and Organizing Ideas: Paraphrasing
    1. Chicago
    2. cell phones
    3. restrooms
    4. children
    5. shower
    6. Ron Nunes
    7. distinguish
    8. public
    9. complained
    10. Elk Grove's
    11. enforce
    12. other
    13. cars
    14. rooms
    15. trouble
    16. searched
    17. called
E. Figuring Out Inferred Meanings
    1. T
    2. T
    3. T
    4. T
    5. T
    6. F
    7. F
F. Thinking Critically
    1. a
    2. c
    3. b
    4. a
G. Building Vocabulary
    Context
    1. d
    2. c
    3. b
    4. b
    5. a
    6. a
    7. d
    Word Parts

1. goes beyond
2. ahead of time
Unusual Words/Unusual Meanings
Answers will vary.
H. Selecting a Learning/Study Strategy
1. d
I. Exploring Ideas Through Discussion and Writing
Answers will vary.
J. Beyond the Classroom to the Web
Answers will vary.

Selection 27 "House Arrest and Electronic Monitoring"
Previewing the Reading
1. house arrest (or) electronic monitoring
2. a. How does electronic monitoring work?
   b. Is there support for electronic monitoring of offenders? (or) What are the benefits of electronic monitoring for offenders?
   c. What are the attitudes of offenders toward electronic monitoring?
   d. How successful is home confinement with electronic monitoring?
A. Understanding the Thesis and Other Main Ideas
1. d
2. a
3. c
4. c
5. b
6. a
7. c
8. d
B. Identifying Details
1. T
2. F
3. F
4. T
5. F
C. Recognizing Methods of Organization and Transitions
1. b
2. c
3. a
4. d
D. Reviewing and Organizing Ideas: Outlining
1. society
2. punishes
3. work
4. future prospects
5. Education
6. prison overcrowding
7. correctional costs
8. Criminal justice
9. national survey
10. conditional
11. low-risk, nondangerous
12. criteria
13. offenders
14. Trial-and-error

269

E. Figuring Out Inferred Meanings
   1. T
   2. T
   3. F
   4. F
   5. T
   6. T
F. Thinking Critically
   1. d
   2. b
   3. c
   4. b
   5. d
G. Building Vocabulary
   Context
   1. b
   2. c
   3. a
   4. c
   5. b
   Word Parts
   1. a person who studies crime
   2. the introduction of new features or ideas
   3. restore themselves to a useful life
   Unusual Words/Unusual Meanings
   1. Answers will vary.
   2. Answers will vary.
A. Selecting a Learning/Study Strategy
   c
B. Exploring Ideas Through Discussion and Writing
   Answers will vary.
C. Beyond the Classroom to the Web
   Answers will vary.

Chapter 20—Health-Related Fields
Selection 28 "Use It and Lose It"
Previewing the Reading
   1. Marilee Arthur
   2. a. How do you squelch starch in your diet?
      b. What does timing have to do with meals?
      c. How do you get out of a workout rut?
A. Understanding the Thesis and Other Main Ideas
   1. b
   2. c
   3. d
   4. a
   5. b
   6. c
   7. d
B. Identifying Details
   1. d
   2. a
   3. d
   4. a
   5. a

C. Recognizing Methods of Organization and Transitions
   1. a
   2. b
D. Reviewing and Organizing Ideas: Mapping
   The answers below appear from top to bottom and from left to right in the diagram.
   1. carbohydrates
   2. fat
   3. protein
   4. energy
   5. muscle
   6. carbohydrates
   7. Too many
   8. glycogen
   9. muscles
   10. liver
   11. fat
E. Figuring Out Inferred Meanings
   1. T
   2. F
   3. T
   4. F
   5. T
F. Thinking Critically
   1. d
   2. b
   3. c
   4. d
G. Building Vocabulary
   Context
   1. b
   2. b
   3. c
   4. a
   5. d
   6. c
   7. d
   8. b
   Word Parts
   1. a person who
   2. not
   3. characteristic of
   4. out
   5. the quality of
   Unusual Words/Unusual Meanings
   1. Answers will vary.
   2. Answers will vary.
   3. Answers will vary.
   4. Answers will vary.
   5. Answers will vary.
H. Selecting a Learning/Study Strategy
   Answers will vary.
I. Exploring Ideas Through Discussion and Writing
   Answers will vary.
J. Beyond the Classroom to the Web
   Answers will vary.

Selection 29 "Make No Mistake: Medical Errors Can Be Deadly Serious"

Previewing the Reading

    1. serious medical mistakes

    2. a. What kinds of mistakes are made in medication?

         b. How do human limitations cause errors? (or) How can human limitations in the medical field be minimized?

         c. How can humans "improve" or prevent medical errors?

A. Understanding the Thesis and Other Main Ideas

    1. c
    2. b
    3. d
    4. a
    5. a
    6. b
    7. c

B. Identifying Details

    1. c
    2. b
    3. b
    4. c
    5. d

C. Recognizing Methods of Organization and Transitions

    1. definition
    2. comparison and contrast
    3. name confusion
    4. for example

D. Reviewing and Organizing Ideas: Paraphrasing

    1. Saturday Night Live
    2. double bypass heart operation
    3. months
    4. father
    5. children
    6. surgeon
    7. artery
    8. operation
    9. sued
    10. surgeon
    11. artery
    12. heart
    13. *People* magazine
    14. mistake
    15. kidney

E. Figuring Out Inferred Meanings

    1. T
    2. F
    3. F
    4. T
    5. T

F. Thinking Critically

    1. c
    2. a
    3. b
    4. d
    5. a

G. Building Vocabulary

    Context

1. c
2. b
3. d
4. a
5. d
6. d
7. b
Word Parts
1. b
2. d
3. a
4. e
5. c
Unusual Words/Unusual Meanings
1. Answers will vary.
2. Answers will vary.
H. Selecting a Learning/Study Strategy
   b
I. Exploring Ideas Through Discussion and Writing
   Answers will vary.
J. Beyond the Classroom to the Web
   Answers will vary.

Selection 30 "Athletes Looking Good and Doing Better with Anabolic Steroids?"

Previewing the Reading
1. anabolic steroids
2. a. What are anabolic steroids?
   b. Why do athletes use anabolic steroids?
   c. What are the risks of anabolic steroid use?
A. Understanding the Thesis and Other Main Ideas
   1. b
   2. c
   3. e
   4. a
   5. b
   6. c
   7. d
B. Identifying Details
   1. 1950s
   2. anemia, muscle atrophy
   3. ten
   4. stacking
   5. 200 mg/day
   6. testosterone
   7. unpredictable
C. Recognizing Methods of Organization and Transitions
   1. b
   2. c
D. Reviewing and Organizing Ideas: Outlining
   1. isometric
   2. body weight
   3. runners
   4. faces
   5. steroid excess
   6. infertility
   7. liver

8. cancer
9. blood cholesterol
10. long-term users
11. coronary heart disease
12. Psychiatric/Mental
13. mental problems
14. Manic
15. personality
16. violence
17. Delusions

E. Figuring Out Inferred Meanings
   1. F
   2. T
   3. F
   4. T

F. Thinking Critically
   1. d
   2. b
   3. c
   4. b
   5. d
   6. a

G. Building Vocabulary
Context
   1. b
   2. c
   3. b
   4. a
   5. c
   6. a
   7. b

Word Parts
   1. d
   2. e
   3. f
   4. a
   5. c
   6. b

Unusual Words/Unusual Meanings
   1. an advantage over their competitor
   2. a decision or agreement
   3. want to be athletes

H. Selecting a Learning/Study Strategy
Answers will vary.

I. Exploring Ideas Through Discussion and Writing
Answers will vary.

J. Beyond the Classroom to the Web
Answers will vary.

Chapter 21 Life Sciences
Selection 31 "Honor Among Beasts"
Previewing the Reading
   1. animal behavior
   2. dogs, monkeys, dolphins, rats, songbirds, coyotes

A. Understanding the Thesis and Other Main Ideas

1. b
2. d
3. c
4. a
5. c
6. a
7. d
8. c

B. Identifying Details
1. F
2. T
3. T
4. F
5. T

C. Recognizing Methods of Organization and Transitions
1. examples
2. for example, in one case, the most obvious example
3. cause and effect
4. however, but

D. Reviewing and Organizing Ideas: Mapping
Dogs and other canines: play bow, cheaters, dishonesty
Monkeys : comfort
Dolphins: exhausted swimmer
Rats: Chirp in laughter
Songbirds: local dialects, nonlocal accents

E. Figuring Out Inferred Meanings
1. T
2. F
3. T

F. Thinking Critically
1. c
2. b
3. b
4. c

G. Building Vocabulary
Context
1. b
2. d
3. c
4. a
5. b
6. d
Word Parts
1. is not able to be believed
2. study of
3. nerves
4. in front of
Unusual Words/Unusual Meanings
Answers will vary.

H. Selecting a Learning/Study Strategy
Answers will vary.

I. Exploring Ideas Through Discussion and Writing
Answers will vary.

J. Beyond the Classroom to the Web
Answers will vary.

Selection 32 "Bugs in Your Pillow"

Previewing the Reading
1. bugs/pillow mites
2. a. Where are the bugs found?
   b. What kind of bugs are they?
   c. What can be done about them?

A. Understanding the Thesis and Other Main Ideas
1. b
2. a
3. c
4. a
5. d
6. b

B. Identifying Details
1. T
2. T
3. F
4. F
5. F
6. T
7. F
8. T
9. T

C. Recognizing Methods of Organization and Transitions
1. d
2. a

D. Reviewing and Organizing Ideas: Paraphrasing
Paragraphs 2 – 3
1. *Dermatophagoides*
2 pillow mite
3. microscope
4. legs
5. neck
6. pads
7. feet
8. filling
Paragraph 6
1. pillow
2. anal pellets
3. Cheyletus
4. breathed

E. Figuring Out Inferred Meanings
1. F
2. F
3. F
4. L
5. L
6. F

F. Thinking Critically
1. c
2. d
3. c
4. b
5. c

276

    6. b

    7. d

G. Building Vocabulary

    Context

    1. b

    2. c

    3. b

    4. a

    5. c

    6. a

    7. b

    8. c

    Word Parts

    1. d

    2. c

    3. b

    4. a

    5. f

    6. g

    7. e

H. Selecting a Learning/Study Strategy

    Answers will vary.

I. Exploring Ideas Through Discussion and Writing

    Answers will vary.

J. Beyond the Classroom to the Web

    Answers will vary.

Selection 33 "The Biodiversity Crisis"

Previewing the Reading

1. species

2. a. What are the three main causes of the biodiversity crisis?

    b. Why does biodiversity matter?

A. Understanding the Thesis and Other Main Ideas

    1. b

    2. c

    3. d

    4. d

    5. c

B. Identifying Details

    1. b

    2. c

    3. d

    4. c

    5. d

C. Recognizing Methods of Organization and Transitions

    1. b

    2. c

    3. a

    4. b

D. Reviewing and Organizing Ideas: Outlining

    1. agriculture

    2. Forestry

    3. Environmental pollution

    4. Introduced Species

    5. native species

6. competition
7. Wildlife
8. commercial
9. Harvesting
10. wildlife products
E. Figuring Out Inferred Meanings
   1. Y
   2. N
   3. Y
   4. Y
   5. Y
   6. N
   7. Y
F. Thinking Critically
   1. b
   2. a
   3. c
   4. disappear
   5. leave
   6. famous
   7. varied
G. Building Vocabulary
   Context
   1. b
   2. c
   3. a
   4. c
   5. a
   6. c
   7. b
   Word Parts
   1. d
   2. f
   3. a
   4. c
   5. b
   6. e
   Unusual Words/Unusual Meanings
   1. Answers will vary.
   2. Answers will vary.
H. Selecting a Learning/Study Strategy
   1. c
I. Exploring Ideas Through Discussion and Writing
   Answers will vary.
J. Beyond the Classroom to the Web
   Answers will vary.

Chapter 22 Physical Sciences/Mathematics
Selection 34 "Are Lotteries Fair?"
Previewing the Reading
   1. the fairness of lotteries
   2. a. Who plays the lottery?
      b. In what ways is the lottery unfair?
      c. What is the evidence for lotteries being unfair?

A. Understanding the Thesis and Other Main Ideas
   1. b
   2. c
   3. a
   4. b
   5. a
B. Identifying Details
   1. c
   2. a
   3. c
   4. b
   5. a
   6. b
   7. b
C. Recognizing Methods of Organization and Transitions
   1. 3, 4, and 6
   2. the cause and effect pattern
D. Reviewing and Organizing Ideas: Paraphrasing
   1. Lotteries
   2. popular
   3. country
   4. Powerball
   5. The Big Game
   6. players
   7. year
   8. counting
   9. winning
   10. advertisements
   11. portray
   12. deal
   13. half
   14. spend
E. Figuring Out Inferred Meanings
   1. F
   2. T
   3. F
   4. T
   5. F
F. Thinking Critically
   1. a
   2. c
   3. d
   4. a
   5. b
G. Building Vocabulary
   Context
   1. b
   2. a
   3. d
   4. d
   Word Parts
   1. put, forth
   2. not
   Unusual Words/Unusual Meanings
   Answers will vary.

H. Selecting a Learning/Study Strategy
   c
I. Exploring Ideas Through Discussion and Writing
   Answers will vary.
J. Beyond the Classroom to the Web
   Answers will vary.

Selection 35 "Is There Life Elsewhere?"
Previewing the Reading
   1. the search for life on other planets
   2. a. Is life on other planets likely?
      b. Why is the search for life important?
      c. How would the discovery of life elsewhere affect us?
A. Understanding the Thesis and Other Main Ideas
   1. c
   2. b
   3. c
   4. a
   5. a
   6. d
B. Identifying Details
   1. Earth
   2. cultures and societies
   3. Astrobiology
   4. Mars and Europa
   5. Cassini
   6. universe
   7. NASA
   8. Carbon-bearing molecules
   9. quickly
   10. conditions
C. Recognizing Methods of Organization and Transitions
   1. c
   2. d
D. Reviewing and Organizing Ideas: Mapping
   The answers below appear from top to bottom and clockwise in the map.
   1. Europa
   2. NASA
   3. Titan, Saturn
   4. intelligent
   5. independent
   6. world
   7. planets
   8. environments
   9. chemical elements
   10. quickly
E. Figuring Out Inferred Meanings
   1. T
   2. F
   3. T
   4. T
   5. T
   6. F
F. Thinking Critically
   1. O

2. F
3. O
4. O
5. F
6. O
G. Building Vocabulary
Context
1. a
2. b
3. b
4. d
Word Parts
1. Earth
2. fit for
H. Selecting a Learning/Study Strategy
1. c
I. Exploring Ideas Through Discussion and Writing
Answers will vary.
J. Beyond the Classroom to the Web.
Answers will vary.

Selection 36 "Air Pollution May Result in Global Warming"
Previewing the Reading
1. how air pollution is causing global warming and affecting the earth's temperature and weather
2. a. What is the greenhouse effect?
   b. What are the effects of global warming?
   c. Why are the effects of global warming uncertain?
A. Understanding the Thesis and Other Main Ideas
1. b
2. d
3. a
4. b
5. a
6. c
7. c
B. Identifying Details
1. a
2. b
3. c
4. b
5. a
6. d
C. Recognizing Methods of Organization and Transitions
1. d
2. b
D. Reviewing and Organizing Ideas: Outlining
1. carbon dioxide and greenhouse
   a. temperature increase
      1. Sun's intensity
2. Ocean's ability to absorb and distribute greenhouse heat
3. a. cloud cover
   b. Atmospheric dust
   c. Aerosols
   d. Ice sheets
E. Figuring Out Inferred Meanings
1. T

2. F
3. T
4. F
5. T
F. Thinking Critically
    1. a
    2. d
    3. c
    4. a
    5. a

G. Building Vocabulary
   Context
    1. d
    2. d
    3. c
    4. a
   Word Parts
    1. light
    2. study
H. Selecting a Learning/Study Strategy
    1. c
I. Exploring Ideas Through Discussion and Writing
   Answers will vary.
J. Beyond the Classroom to the Web
   Answers will vary.

Chapter 23 Workplace/Career Fields
Selection 37 "Building Toward a Career"
Previewing the Reading
    1. finding a job you are suited for
    2. a. How can you find out what you have to offer employers?
       b. How can you discover what you want to do?
       c. How can you make yourself valuable to employers?
A. Understanding the Thesis and Other Main Ideas
    1. b
    2. c
    3. c
    4. d
    5. d
B. Identifying Details
    1. T
    2. F
    3. T
    4. F
    5. T
C. Recognizing Methods of Organization and Transitions
    1. c
    2. d
D. Reviewing and Organizing Ideas: Summarizing
    1. college
    2. job
    3. three
    4. employers
    5. portfolio

6. perform
7. temporary
8. skills

E. Figuring Out Inferred Meanings
   1. T
   2. F
   3. T
   4. T
   5. F
   6. F
   7. T
   8. T

F. Thinking Critically
   1. a
   2. b
   3. d
   4. c
   5. a

G. Building Vocabulary
   Context
   1. b
   2. a
   3. a
   4. d
   5. c
   Word Parts
   1. outside of
   2. picture
   Unusual Words/Unusual Meanings
   Answers will vary.

H. Selecting a Learning /Study Strategy
   1. b

I. Exploring Ideas Through Discussion and Writing
   Answers will vary.

J. Beyond the Classroom to the Web
   Answers will vary.

Selection 38 "Rx for Anger at Work"

Previewing the Reading
   1. anger at work
   2. a. What makes us angry at work?
        b. Is there such a thing as bad anger?
        c. How can you avoid feeling out of control when you are angry?

A. Understanding the Thesis and Other Main Ideas
   1. d
   2. a
   3. c
   4. a
   5. c

B. Identifying Details
   1. F
   2. T
   3. F
   4. T
   5. F

C. Recognizing Methods of Organization and Transitions
1. b
2. c
A. Reviewing and Organizing Ideas: Outlining
1. Work situations that provoke anger
2. The critical boss
3. promotion
4. Being maligned by coworkers
5. incompetent boss
6. Paul Meier
7. illegitimate anger
8. Perfectionism
9. *The Portable Therapist*
10. Cool your anger with humor
B. Figuring Out Inferred Meanings
1. T
2. F
3. F
4. F
5. T
6. T
7. T
C. Thinking Critically
1. d
2. b
3. b
4. c
5. b
D. Building Vocabulary
Context
1. b
2. a
3. c
4. b
5. d
6. a
7. b
Word Parts
1. d   in
2. c   ir
3. b   in
4. a   il
5. g   un
6. h   in
7. e   in
8. f   in
Unusual Words/Unusual Meanings
1. Answers will vary.
2. Answers will vary.
3. Answers will vary.
4. Answers will vary.
5. Answers will vary.
E. Selecting a Learning/Study Strategy
Answers will vary.
F. Exploring Ideas Through Discussion and Writing
Answers will vary.

284

G. Beyond the Classroom to the Web
Answers will vary.

Selection 28 "The Sandman Is Dead—Long Live the Sleep Deprived Walking Zombie"

Previewing the Reading
1. sleep or sleep deprivation
2. a. Why is sleep important?
    b. How much sleep do we need?
    c. How much sleep are we getting?
    d. What are the effects of sleeplessness?

A. Understanding the Thesis and Other Main Ideas
1. c
2. b
3. d
4. c
5. e
6. b
7. a

B. Identifying Details
1. d
2. d
3. b
4. b
5. c

C. Recognizing Methods of Organization and Transitions
1. b
2. d

D. Reviewing and Organizing Ideas: Mapping
The answers below appear from top to bottom and from left to right in the map.
1. 31% have fallen asleep
2. $30 billion each year
3. too sleepy at work
4. One-third
5. 56% fall asleep on the job once a week
6. Health costs

E. Figuring Out Inferred Meanings
1. T
2. F
3. T
4. F

F. Thinking Critically
1. c
2. d
3. c
4. d
5. d
6. b
7. a

G. Building Vocabulary
Context
1. c
2. d
3. c
4. a

5. d
6. c
7. a
Word Parts
1. creative
2. state or condition
3. able to
Unusual Words/Unusual Meanings
1. Answers will vary.
2. Answers will vary.
H. Selecting a Learning/Study Strategy
    1. d
I. Exploring Ideas Through Discussion and Writing
    Answers will vary.
J. Beyond the Classroom to the Web
    Answers will vary.

PART THREE: TEXTBOOK CHAPTER READINGS ANSWER KEY
<u>Chapter 24 – Psychology Textbook Chapter</u>
Psychology Selection 1 "Roles and Rules" (pages 296-304)
Before Reading
Previewing the Section
    1. roles and rules
    2. a. What was the obedience study?
        b. What was the prison study?
        c. What power do roles have?

After Reading
A. Understanding Main Ideas
    1. d
    2. c
    3. d
B. Identifying Details
    1. norms
    2. two-thirds
    3. situation
    4. were not
    5. disappointed
C. Recognizing Methods of Organization and Transitions
    1. a
    2. b
D. Reviewing and Organizing Ideas: Mapping
    The answers below appear from top to bottom and from left to right in the diagram.
    1. authority
    2. responsibility
    3. commitment
    4. investment
    5. Routinization
    6. behavior
    7. good manners
    8. rude
E. Figuring Out Inferred Meanings
    1. T
    2. F
    3. F

4. F
5. T
F. Thinking Critically
1. d
2. a
3. d
4. b
5. c
G. Building Vocabulary
Context
1. b
2. c
3. b
4. c
5. c
6. a
7. d
8. c
Word Parts
1. f
2. e
3. d
4. b
5. c
6. a
Unusual Words/Unusual Meanings
1. Answers will vary.
2. Answers will vary.
H. Selecting a Learning/Study Strategy
Answers will vary.
I. Exploring Ideas Through Discussion and Writing
Answers will vary.

Psychology Selection 2 "Identity, Attributions, and Attitudes" (pages 304-311)
Before Reading
Previewing the Section
1. identity, attributions, and attitudes
2. a. What is self-identity?
    b. What are attributions?
    c. Where do attitudes come from?
    d. What is friendly persuasion?
    e. What is coercive persuasion?
After Reading
A. Understanding Main Ideas
1. d
2. c
3. c
4. a
5. d
6. c
B. Identifying Details
1. T
2. F
3. T
4. T
5. F

C. Recognizing Methods of Organization and Transitions
    1. a
    2. b
    3. c
    4. d
    5. a
D. Reviewing and Organizing Ideas: Mapping
    The answers below appear from top to bottom and from left to right in the diagram.
    1. Weak
    2. Strong
    3. Weak
    4. Assimilated
E. Figuring Out Inferred Meanings
    1. S
    2. D
    3. D
    4. S
    5. S
    6. D
    7. S
    8. D
F. Thinking Critically
    1. c
    2. c
    3. c
G. Building Vocabulary
    Context
    1. c
    2. b
    3. a
    4. b
    5. c
    6. c
    7. a
    8. d
    9. c
    10. d
    Word Parts
    1. two
    2. many
    3. outside or beyond
H. Selecting a Learning/Study Strategy
    Answers will vary.
I. Exploring Ideas Through Discussion and Writing
    Answers will vary.

Psychology Selection 3 "Individuals in Groups" (pages 311-317)
Before Reading
Previewing the Section
    1. how individuals behave in groups
    2. a. What is conformity?
       b. What is groupthink?
       c. What is meant by the "anonymous crowd"?
       d. What does courage have to do with nonconformity?
A. Understanding Main Ideas
    1. b

2. d
3. c
4. c
5. c
6. b
B. Identifying Details
1. decreased
2. less
3. direct
4. encourage
5. decreases
6. increases
7. less
C. Recognizing Methods of Organization and Transitions
1. b
2. c
D. Reviewing and Organizing Ideas: Summarizing
1. independent
2. need
3. justify
4. act
5. World War II
6. concentration camp
7. employees
8. demands
9. work
10. cities
E. Figuring Out Inferred Meanings
1. T
2. T
3. F
4. T
F. Thinking Critically
1. d
2. b
3. c
4. c
G. Building Vocabulary
Context
1. b
2. c
3. b
4. c
5. c
6. a
7. d
8. c
9. d
10. b
Word Parts
1. not able to be easily attacked
2. a person who agrees
3. the condition of not being an individual
Unusual Words/Unusual Meanings
1. Answers will vary.
2. Answers will vary.

3. Answers will vary.
H. Selecting a Learning/Study Strategy
   Answers will vary.
I. Exploring Ideas Through Discussion and Writing
   Answers will vary.

Psychology Selection 4 "Cross-Cultural Relations" (pages 317-331)
Before Reading
Previewing the Section
   1. cross-cultural relations
2. a. What are stereotypes?
   b. What is prejudice?
   c. What are the origins of prejudice?
   d. What are the varieties of prejudice?
   e. Can cultures get along? (or) How can cultures get along?

After Reading
A. Understanding Main Ideas
   1. d
   2. a
   3. d
   4. c
   5. d
   6. b
   7. d
B. Identifying Details
   1. increasing
   2. less
   3. negative
   4. increases
   5. decreasing
C. Recognizing Methods of Organization and Transitions
   1. a
   2. b
D. Reviewing and Organizing Ideas: Outlining
   1. discrimination
   2. rights
   3. Women's
   4. Contact
   5. get acquainted
   6. cooperation
E. Figuring Out Inferred Meanings
   1. T
   2. T
   3. T
   4. F
F. Thinking Critically
   1. d
   2. b
   3. b
   4. d
   5. d
G. Building Vocabulary
   Context
   1. b
   2. a
   3. c

4. b
5. c
6. c
7. a
8. d
9. c
10. d
11. b
12. c

Word Parts

1. c
2. a
3. b
4. g
5. f
6. d
7. e

Unusual Words/Unusual Meanings

1. Answers will vary.
2. Answers will vary.

H. Selecting a Learning/Study Strategy
   Answers will vary.
I. Exploring Ideas Through Discussion and Writing
   Answers will vary.

Chapter 25 – Biology Textbook Chapter Answer Key

Biology Selection 1 "Overview of Animal Nutrition" (pages 485-488)

Before Reading

Previewing the Section

1. a. animal diets
    b. stages of food processing
    c. digesting compartments

After Reading

A. Understanding Main Ideas
   1. b
   2. c
   3. b
   4. a
   5. d
B. Identifying Details
   1. T
   2. F
   3. T
   4. T
   5. F
   6. T
   7. T
C. Recognizing Methods of Organization and Transitions
   1. d
   2. a
   3. d
D. Reviewing and Organizing Ideas: Summarizing
   1. chemical digestion
   2. food vacuoles
   3. digestive enzymes

    4. digestive sacs
    5. undigested wastes
    6. digestive tubes
E. Figuring Out Inferred Meanings
    1. F
    2. F
    3. T
    4. T
    5. T
F. Thinking Critically
    1. b
    2. c
    3. b
    4. a
    5. d
G. Building Vocabulary
    Context
    1. b
    2. a
    3. c
    4. b
    5. a
    6. c
    7. b
    8. d
    9. a
    Word Parts
    1. c
    2. g
    3. f
    4. e
    5. b
    6. a
    7. d
H. Selecting a Learning/Study Strategy
    Answers will vary.
I. Exploring Ideas Through Discussion and Writing
    Answers will vary.

Biology Selection 2 "A Tour of the Human Digestive System (pages 489-494)
Before Reading
Previewing the Section
    1. a. mouth
       b. pharynx
       c. esophagus
       d. stomach
       e. small intestine
       f. large intestine
After Reading
A. Understanding Main Ideas
    1. c
    2. d
    3. b
    4. c
    5. c
    6. a

      7. d
B. Identifying Details
      1. T
      2. F
      3. F
      4. T
      5. T
      6. T
      7. F
C. Recognizing Methods of Organization and Transitions
      1. b
      2. a
      3. a
      4. d
D. Reviewing and Organizing Ideas: Mapping
      1.   Mouth: Mechanical, saliva
      2.   Pharynx: trachea/windpipe
      3.   Esophagus: peristalsis
      4.   Stomach: acid chyme
      5.   Small intestine: nutrients
      6.   Large Intestine: the colon, The rectum
E. Figuring Out Inferred Meanings
      1. N
      2. Y
      3. Y
      4. Y
      5. N
      6. Y
F. Thinking Critically
      1. a
      2. b
      3. d
      4. c
G. Building Vocabulary
    Context
      1. b
      2. d
      3. a
      4. c
      5. c
      6. b
      7. a
    Word Parts
      1. c
      2. e
      3. a
      4. f
      5. b
      6. d
    Unusual Words/Unusual Meanings
    Answers will vary.
H. Selecting a Learning/Study Strategy
    Answers will vary.
I. Exploring Ideas Through Discussion and Writing
    Answers will vary.

Biology Selection 3 "Human Nutritional Requirements" and "Nutritional Disorders" (pages 494-500)

Before Reading

Previewing the Section

    1. a. How does the body use food as fuel?

         b. What nutrients are essential to a healthy diet?

         c. What are malnutrition and obesity?

A. Understanding Main Ideas

    1. c

    2. a

    3. b

    4. d

    5. a

    6. a

    7. b

    8. c

B. Identifying Details

    1. more

    2. smaller

    3. more

    4. rare

    5. animal

    6. increases

C. Recognizing Methods of Organization and Transitions

    1. b

    2. b

    3. c

    4. b

D. Reviewing and Organizing Ideas: Outlining

The answers below appear from top to bottom and from left to right in the diagram.

      A. 1. your food

           2. expend

      B. 3. stress level, heredity

   II. Building Material

      A. Proteins

      C. Minerals

   III. Food Labels

        1. weight

E. Figuring Out Inferred Meanings

    1. F

    2. T

    3. F

    4. F

    5. T

    6. T

F. Thinking Critically

    1. d

    2. c

    3. b

    4. b

    5. c

    6. c

G. Building Vocabulary

Context

    1. d

2. c
3. b
4. a
5. c
6. a
7. d
Word Parts
1. c
2. e
3. a
4. g
5. b
6. d
7. f
8. j
9. h
10. i
H. Selecting a Learning/Study Strategy
    Answers will vary.
I. Exploring Ideas Through Discussion and Writing
    Answers will vary.

Answer Key to Quizzes in the Instructor's Manual

Chapter 11: Social Sciences
Selection 1. Urban Legends (p. 79)
1. T
2. T
3. F
4. c
5. b

Selection 2. The New Flirting Game (p. 82)
1. F
2. T
3. T
4. c
5. d

Selection 3. Coming into My Own (p. 84)
1. T
2. F
3. F
4. d
5. a

Chapter 12: Communication/Speech
Selection 4. Reality TV: Race to the Bottom (p. 87)
a. F
b. F
c. T
d. d
e. c

Selection 5. War: The Mother of All Words (p. 89)
1. T
2. T
3. T
4. c
5. d

Selection 6. Lovers (p. 92)
1. T
2. F
3. F
4. a
5. d

Chapter 13: Anthropology
Selection 7. To Love and to Cherish (p. 95)
1. T
2. F
3. T
4. b
5. b

Selection 8. Peti's Malu: Traditons of Samoan Tattooing (p. 97)
1. F
2. T
3. T
4. d
5. a

Section 9. Play, Leisure, and Culture (p. 100)
1. T
2. T
3. F
4. c
5. b

Chapter 14: Education
Selection 10. Should Students Attend School Year Round? Yes (p. 104)
1. T
2. T
3. F
4. d
5. b
Selection 11. Should Students Attend School Year Round? No (p. 107)
1. F
2. T
3. T
4. a
5. d
Selection 12. His Name Is Michael (p. 110)
1. T
2. F
3. T
4. d
5. b

Chapter 15: Arts/Humanities/Literature
Selection 13. Nampeyo: Shaping Her People's Heritage (1852-1942) (p. 113)
1. F
2. F
3. F
4. c
5. b
Selection 14. Gregory (p. 115)
1. F
2. T
3. T
4. a
5. d
Selection 15. The Truth Is (p. 117)
1. F
2. T
3. F
4. c
5. b

Chapter 16: Public Policy/Contemporary Issues
Selection 16. The Effects of the Minimum Wage (p. 120)
1. T
2. F
3. T
4. b
5. a

Selection 17. When Living Is a Fate Worse Than Death (p. 123)
    1. T
    2. F
    3. F
    4. c
    5. a

Selection 18. Seoul Searching (p. 126)
    1. T
    2. F
    3. F
    4. b
    5. d

Chapter 18: Political Science/Government/History

Selection 19. The Beautiful Laughing Sisters—An Arrival Story (p. 129)
    1. F
    2. T
    3. F
    4. a
    5. c

Selection 20. Profile of a Terrorist (p. 132)
    1. T
    2. F
    3. T
    4. c
    5. b

Selection 21. Whether to Vote: A Citizen's First Choice (p. 135)
    1. F
    2. T
    3. F
    4. d
    5. a

Chapter 18: Business/Advertising/Economics

Selection 22. Four Simple Words That Guarantee the Job of Your Dreams (p. 137)
    1. F
    2. F
    3. T
    4. b
    5. a

Selection 23. McDonald's Makes a Lot of People Angry for a Lot of Different Reasons (p. 139)
    1. T
    2. T
    3. F
    4. b
    5. b

Selection 24. Hispanic Americans: A Growing Market Segment (p. 141)
    1. F
    2. F
    3. T
    4. c
    5. a

Chapter 19: Technology/Computers

Selection 25. Blogger Beware (p. 143)
        1.   T
        2.   T
        3.   F
        4.   a
        5.   a

Selection 26. Hold It Right There, and Drop That Camera (p. 145)
        1.   F
        2.   F
        3.   T
        4.   b
        5.   d

Selection 27. House Arrest and Electronic Monitoring (p. 147)
        1.   F
        2.   F
        3.   T
        4.   c
        5.   b

Chapter 20: Health-Related Fields

Selection 28. Use It and Lose It (p. 150)
        1.   T
        2.   T
        3.   F
        4.   a
        5.   a

Selection 29. Make No Mistake: Medical Errors Can Be Deadly Serious (p. 153)
        1.   F
        2.   T
        3.   T
        4.   b
        5.   c

Selection 30. Athletes Looking Good and Doing Better with Anabolic Steroids? (p. 156)
        1.   F
        2.   F
        3.   T
        4.   a
        5.   c

Chapter 21: Life Sciences

Selection 31. Honor Among Beasts (p. 159)
        1.   T
        2.   T
        3.   F
        4.   c
        5.   c

Selection 32. Bugs in Your Pillow (p. 161)
        1.   T
        2.   F
        3.   F
        4.   a
        5.   a

Selection 33. The Biodiversity Crisis (p. 165)
        1.   F
        2.   T
        3.   F
        4.   c
        5.   a

Chapter 22 Physical Sciences/Mathematics
Selection 34. Are Lotteries Fair? (p. 168)
        1.   T
        2.   F
        3.   F
        4.   C
        5.   B
Selection 35. Is There Life Elsewhere? (p. 171)
        1.   F
        2.   T
        3.   F
        4.   b
        5.   c
Selection 36. Air Pollution May Result in Global Warming (p. 174)
        1.   T
        2.   T
        3.   F
        4.   b
        5.   d

Chapter 23: Workplace/Career Fields
Selection 37. Building Toward a Career (p. 176)
        1.   F
        2.   F
        3.   T
        4.   c
        5.   a
Selection 38. Rx for Anger at Work (p. 179)
        1.   F
        2.   T
        3.   T
        4.   a
        5.   b
Selection 39. The Sandman Is Dead—Long Live the Sleep Deprived Walking Zombie (p. 181)
        1.   F
        2.   T
        3.   F
        4.   b
        5.   b

Chapter 24: *Psychology Chapter*
Reading 1. Roles and Rules (p. 183)
        1.   T
        2.   F
        3.   F
        4.   c
        5.   a

Reading 2. Identity, Attribution, and Attitudes (p. 187)
  1. T
  2. F
  3. T
  4. c
  5. c
Reading 3. Individuals in Groups (p. 191)
  1. F
  2. F
  3. T
  4. d
  5. c
Reading 4. Cross-Cultural Relations (p. 196)
  1. T
  2. F
  3. T
  4. d
  5. a

Chapter 25. *Biology Chapter*
Reading 1. Overview of Animal Nutrition (p. 201)
  1. F
  2. T
  3. F
  4. d
  5. a
Reading 2. A Tour of the Human Digestive System (p. 205)
  1. F
  2. F
  3. F
  4. c
  5. c
Reading 3. Human Nutritional Requirements and Nutritional Disorders (p. 209)
  1. F
  2. T
  3. T
  4. a
  5. b

Part VI: Appendix

Tips for Reading the Social Sciences

- **Pay attention to terminology.** (Learn terms that describe behavior, name stages and processes and label principles, theories, and models. Learn the names of researchers and theories. Learn to highlight and transfer to index cards or vocabulary log.)

- **Understand explanations and theories.** (As you learn how people behave as they do, ask: "What behavior is being explained? What evidence is offered that it is correct? Of what use is this explanation?"

- **Look for supporting evidence.** (Notice details, examples, anecdotes, or research evidence.)

- **Make comparisons and connections.** (Notice relationships and comparisons; draw connections between topics.)

- **Make practical applications.** (Consider how the information is useful to you in real-life situations. Make marginal notes of situations that illustrate what you are reading about.)

Tips for Reading
Communication/Speech

- **Pay attention to process.**

- **Pay attention to principles—rules that govern how communication works.**

- **Notice theories** (explanations that attempt to describe how or why something happens).

- **Be alert for cultural differences.** (Not all cultures and ethnic groups follow the same conventions and theories.)

- **Pay attention to terminology.**

- **Think critically.** (Ask challenging questions.)

Tips for Reading Anthropology

- **Pay attention to terminology.** (Learn the names of important researchers and theorists.)

- **Focus on patterns of behavior.** (Identify patterns. People in separate cultures often differ not only in how they behave, but also in how they think.)

- **Make comparisons between and among groups and cultures.** (Look for relationships and make comparisons. Draw charts or maps that compare practices, beliefs, or family structures.)

- **Make practical applications.** (Relate what you read to real-life situations.

Tips for Reading in the Field of Education

- Pay attention to issues. (Education is a field that often involves controversy. Current issues include school vouchers, security within schools, teacher and student competencies.)

- Realize that measurement and assessment are important.

- Look for trends and innovations.

- Pay attention to multicultural aspects of education.

Tips for Reading the Arts/Humanities/Literature

Focus on values. (Ask yourself why the work or piece is valuable and important.)

Pay attention to the medium. (Words, sound, canvas, and clay are all means through which artistic expression occurs.)

Look for a message or an interpretation. (Works of art and literature express meaning and create a feeling or impression.)

Read literature slowly and carefully. (Rereading may be necessary. Pay attention to the writer's choice of words, descriptions, comparisons, and arrangement of ideas.)

Tips for Reading about Public Policy and Contemporary Issues

- **Read critically.** (Controversial issues are often presented as opinion, not fact.)

- **Look for reasons that support a position.** (Examine the author's motive for taking a stance on an issue.)

- **Consider opposing viewpoints.** (Always look at the other side of the issue.)

Tips for Reading Political Science/Government/History

- **Focus on the significance of events, both current and historical.** (What are the immediate and long-range effects?.)

- **Analyze motivations.** (What causes people and groups to take political action?)

- **Consider political organizations.** (How and why do people organize themselves into political groups and parties?)

- **Be alert for bias and partisanship.**

- **Sort facts from opinions.** (Opinions and historical interpretation need to be evaluated.)

Tips for Reading Business/Advertising and Economics

- **Focus on process.** (Management, marketing, finance, statistics, retailing, information systems, and organizational labor are concerned with processes.)

- **Focus on the theme of globalization.** (Growing numbers of U.S. businesses are competing in foreign markets.)

- **Consider ethical decision-making and social responsibility.** (The application of moral standards to business activity and operation is of increasing importance in field of business.)

Tips for Reading about Technology/Computers

◆ **Read Slowly.** (Technical material tends to be factually dense and requires careful, slow reading.)

◆ **Notice Technical Vocabulary.** (Context clues will be helpful.)

◆ **Focus on the Process.** (Technical writing focuses on how things work.)

◆ **Use Visualization.** (Imagine the process or procedure as you read it and you will improve your ability to recall details.)

Tips for Reading in Health-Related Fields

- **Learn the necessary terminology.** (Reading in the field and speaking with health-care professionals will be easier if you master the specialize vocabulary.)

- **Learn about the basic human body systems.** (You have to know how your body works in order to take care of it and to understand the readings in the field.)

- **Read critically.** (Notice many different viewpoints and proposed cures.)

Tips for Reading the Life Sciences

- **Adopt a scientific mind set.** (Get in the habit of asking questions and seeking answers, analyzing problems, and looking for solutions or explanations.)

- **Learn new terminology.** (Science is exact and precise, and scientists use specific terminology to make communication as error-free as possible.)

- **Focus on cause-effect and process.** (Since science is concerned with how and why things happen, recognizing cause-effect and process can be critical.)

Tips for Reading the Physical Sciences/ Mathematics

- **Read slowly and reread if necessary.** (Both mathematics and the physical sciences are very technical and detailed.)

- **Focus on new terminology.** (Mathematics and physical science are exact and precise. Learn the language of science.)

- **Use writing to learn.** (Highlighting and annotating are not sufficient. Express ideas in your own words. If you cannot do this, you probably do not understand it.)

Tips for Reading about the Workplace/Career Fields

- **Focus on practical information.** (Try to find techniques and strategies to help you on the job or in your job search.)

- **Pay attention to trends and projections.** (Read to find how to make yourself marketable and competitive.)

- **Apply what you learn.** (Use metacognition and make connections to find out how the information will help you.)

Book Review Project

- **Title:**
- **Author:**
- **Publisher and Publication Date:**
- **Number of Pages:**
- **Rating:** *(Excellent; Very Good; Good; Fair, Poor)*
- **Themes:**
- **Page Number of Brief Passage to Read Aloud:**
- **Summary:** A succinct synopsis of the story, including one direct quotation from the book.
- **Evaluation:** A one-paragraph critique that expresses your opinion of the book, who it would appeal to, and what you liked or disliked. Be sure to justify your rating.

Book Project Grading

- **Written Review**=20 points
- **Presentation**=40 points
- **Following Directions and Meeting Deadlines**=10 points
- **Total Project**=100 points

- **Written Project**:
- **Themes**=10 points
- **Summary**=20 points. (This should include who, what, when, where, why, and how. Also, the student will include a topic sentence in each paragraph with specific supporting details and transition words when applicable. Extra points can be accrued for appropriate use of vocabulary words, which should be highlighted or underlined in the body of the paper. No credit will be given for plagiarized work.)

- **Opinion**=20 points. (The student will justify his or her rating with specific observations on the book by including a topic sentence, and details connected with transition words. Extra credit will be given when vocabulary words are used appropriately and highlighted or underlined.

In the summary or in the opinion, you must include a direct quotation from the book.

- **Presentation**: In 2-3 minutes share your summary without revealing the ending and read a brief passage from the book. Be prepared to field questions.

Book Review Sample

Many Waters
By Madeleine L'Engle
Farrar, Straus, Giroux, 1986
310 Pages
Very Good
Good versus Evil; Hubris; Synchronicity; Love; Family Relationships
Page 227

When fifteen-year-old twins Sandy and Dennys Murray playfully punch a message into their father's computer, they only imagine an escape from the New England snowstorm. They type, "Take me someplace warm. Someplace sparsely populated. Low humidity." Whoosh! Unwittingly, the boys tesser (travel through time and space) to Noah's pre-flood desert. There they find a land unbearably hot with little water; a land populated with mammoths and manticores; a land guarded by seraphim and tainted by nephilim; a land free of disease and pollution, where stars hang low and seem to sing. Still, terrorism exists, volcanoes erupt, and earthquakes rumble.

All of the characters from the Genesis story are there and L'Engle has added a few: four daughters to Noah. Sandy and Dennys realize they are in Noah's desert for a purpose. Knowing they cannot tamper with historical events is difficult since they both love Yalith, the youngest daughter—a character, they recall, who was not on the Ark.

This is a very good book, which directs questions on good and evil as well as God's purpose for man and his role in man's life. The book, however, is not without flaws. First, because of their innocence, the twins are able to speak the "Old Language." This seems a bit contrived. Also, the book contains a painfully graphic description of a birth. Finally, some readers may find the manner in which one of Noah's daughters escapes the flood is less than credible.

L'Engle once said that a good writer should make the reader think. She does this. By unveiling a truth and asking, "What if?", she gives the reader imaginings that are never disappointing.

Resources

Albom, Mitch, *Tuesdays with Morrie,* New York, Doubleday, 1997.

Carson, Benjamin, MD., with Gregg Lewis, *The Big Picture,* Grand Rapids, MI, Zondervan PublishingHouse, 1999.

Carson, Benjamin, MD, with Cecil Murphy, *Think Big,* Grand Rapids, MI, Zondervan Publishing House, 1992

Covey, Stephen, *The Seven Habits of Highly Effective People,* New York, Simon and Schuster, 1990.

Daniels, Harvey, *Literature Circles: Voice and Choice in the Student-Centered Classroom,* York, ME, Stenhouse Publishers, 1994.

Silberman, Mel, *Active Learning: 101 Strategies to Teach Any Subject,* Boston, Allyn and Bacon, 1996.